The Fighting Staff

The Fighting Staff

Dwight C. McLemore

PALADIN PRESS • BOULDER, COLORADO

Also by Dwight C. McLemore

Advanced Bowie Techniques
Bowie and Big-Knife Fighting Book
Fighting Sword
Fighting Tomahawk
Fighting Tomahawk: The Video

The Fighting Staff
by Dwight C. McLemore

Copyright © 2009 by Dwight C. McLemore

ISBN 13: 978-1-58160-714-7
Printed in the United States of America

Published by Paladin Press, a division of
Paladin Enterprises, Inc.
Gunbarrel Tech Center
7077 Winchester Circle
Boulder, Colorado 80301 USA
+1.303.443.7250

Direct inquiries and/or orders to the above address.

Visit our website at www.paladin-press.com

TABLE OF CONTENTS

Table of Contents

To Grand Master Hoy K. Lee, whose leadership and professionalism started me on this road so many, many years ago.

WARNING

Misuse of the information and techniques in this book could result in serious injury or death. The author, publisher, and distributor of this text disclaim any liability from damage or injuries of any type that a reader or user of the information may incur. The techniques should never be attempted or practiced without the direct supervision of a qualified weapons instructor. Moreover, it is the reader's responsibility to research and comply with all local, state, and federal laws and regulations pertaining to possession, carry, and use of weapons. This text is *for academic study only.*

PREFACE

Although I am generally associated with the bowie knife and tomahawk, the fact is that I have actually been studying and training with the staff for much longer than with either of these weapons. Since that day back in 1996 when my kung fu teacher, Grand Master Hoy Lee, introduced me to the Chinese "double-headed staff," the spirit of this crude and simple weapon has been with me. The gift that Sifu gave me was more than just a set of techniques in an Asian fighting art; he bestowed on me an understanding of conceptual principles that could be applied to other martial skills.

As I moved into the Western martial arts and opened my own school, those staff principles seemed to continuously surface as part of the curriculum—like an old friend who was always ready to help out. My study of medieval and Renaissance fight manuals was made easier because of the background I had acquired of this weapon.

While the staff is deceptively simple in the basic techniques, there always seems to be some new application or method that appears to open one's mind. This manual is not about this or that specific staff system, nor does it attempt to duplicate some method of the past. What is reflected here is a hybrid system that borrows heavily from the Chinese, Korean, and European martial arts through the ages. During the preparation of this text, I was not interested in how this or that Asian or European master executed a specific technique. Although I've sprinkled some relevant historical information throughout the text, I really am more interested in the application of fighting techniques to today's world.

That said, within these pages I do not favor the work of any particular system or martial discipline. This is simply my take on a lot of different approaches. This is a fundamental workbook that applies a modern slant on some old concepts. I would like for you to think of this as a basic workbook to take to the training hall and begin your study with. Write all over the pages and use it as a guide to developing your own method for your own martial journey.

ORGANIZATION AND USE

This manual is broken down into a series of 25 training objectives that focus on the fundamentals of fighting with the staff. Around each of these objectives, I include some techniques and conceptual aspects that will, for all practical purposes, serve as a "language" for more advanced training. To present the skills and techniques, I use three illustrative approaches. In Figure 1, you are looking at an opponent from the user's viewpoint. The technique is illustrated by showing a "floating staff" that gives a perspective into where the weapon is moving.

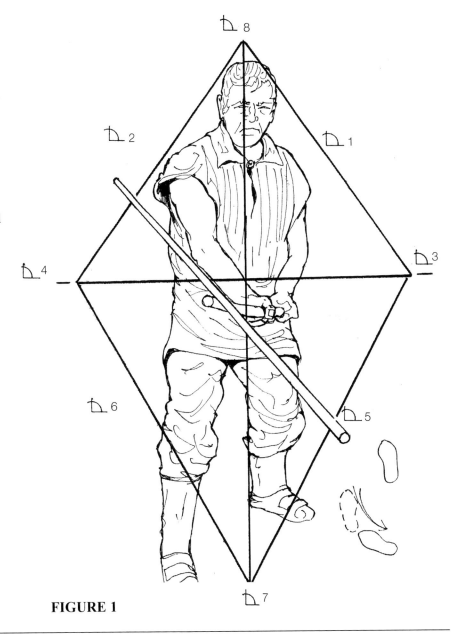

FIGURE 1

The typical side view of the technique will also be used along with a three-quarter view in some cases. This approach is demonstrated in Figure 2.

FIGURE 2

An overhead view of the staff movement and associated footwork patterns will be used when necessary. Throughout these illustrations you will see footprints illustrating the footwork related to the technique or drill. The initial position is indicated by dashed footprints, while the final location is indicated by a solid line. An example is included in Figure 3.

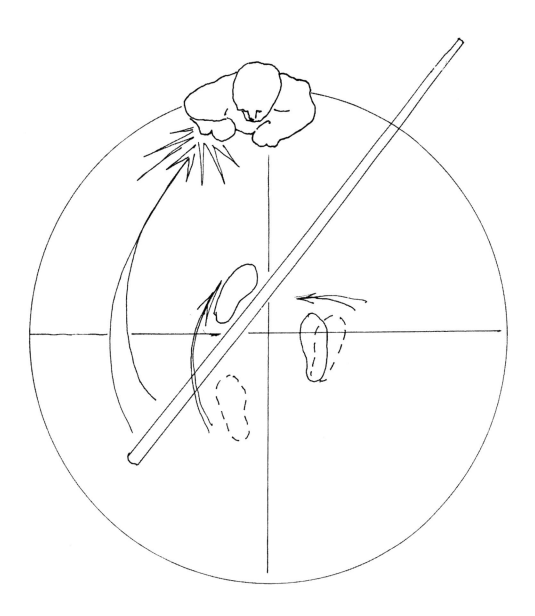

FIGURE 3

CHAPTER 1
ASPECTS OF THE STAFF

WHAT IS A STAFF?

The staff sat in the corner of my training hall for more than three years. Through all our moves, my wife and I had handled it like a piece of furniture, moving it from place to place. Usually it ended up being propped up against the wall in the garage, where it remained till it got loaded up again for another move. It saw a lot of use during the early years when I trained with Sifu Hoy K. Lee in Jow Ga Kung Fu and later as part of the curriculum of the School of Two Swords. The 7-foot staff was stained from grit, sweat, and oils from my hands, and gave the normally white wax wood a spotty tan varnish. You might say that those training sessions had forced enough DNA into that big stick to make it a member of the family. Indeed, it was part of me.

These thoughts came to mind when I stumbled across that staff while cleaning out the garage recently. As I picked it up and wiped off a two-year layer of dust, my wife, Jeneene, came up to me and asked, "Is that your staff? Boy! You've had that a long time, haven't you?" I explained how the wood had come from China and been used to fashion fighting sticks and spear shafts for thousands of years, relating the story of how wax wood would absorb the oils and sweat from the user and become part of him. She smiled, turned the stick over in her hands, and tossed it back to me. "I love that tale. You know, now that you've got that sword book out of the way, you should do something on this."

Well, I took my wife's advice, and the product is the book you are holding now.

The term *staff* is generally defined as a long club that is employed with two hands. Staff weapons are known to have existed throughout history in both Western and Asian cultures. They have been called by many names—for example, the stave and quarterstaff in European cultures, and pole and long stick in Asia. China, Korea, Japan, Philippines, Okinawa, and East India, and the European continent all developed and practiced techniques for staff-like weapons that ranged from 4 to 12 feet in length.

Overall the staff is probably one of man's oldest weapons; it was initially used for personal defense and later as a training vehicle for a variety of polearms associated with the formations of 12th- to 17th-century combat. The staff was a folk weapon of the common people and the lowly footman. Offensive and defensive techniques usually consist of striking, levering, thrusting, and blocking. The staff can be used at long, medium, and close ranges.

Historically, staff weapons never received the literary attention that the sword did. Although many masters taught fighting with staff weapons, only brief sections on their use can be found in fight books prior to the 17th century. Today we do not have this problem, because there are many books and videos that address both the history and use of the staff. That said, I will not discuss the generic history of staff techniques; plenty of reference works already fill that need. Instead, I will sprinkle some of the more significant historical aspects that I adapted into the fighting techniques.

The fighting techniques depicted in this manual

are hybrid, combining both modern and historical methods. In some cases, I mixed both European and Asian techniques together to arrive at a reasonably effective approach that would realistically work. As I mentioned in the preface, I make no claim to being historically accurate; rather I have attempted to learn from the past rather than to replicate it.

LENGTH

"[Y]ou shall stand upright, holding the staff upright close by your body, with your left hand, reaching with your right hand your staff as high as you can, and then allow to that length a space to set both your hands, when you come to fight, wherein you may conveniently strike, thrust, and ward, and that is the just length to be made according to your stature."

George Silver, 1599

Basically what "Ole George" is telling us is that the length of a staff is determined by one's height. The Chinese and the German teachers favored staffs up to 12 feet in length, which may well have been used when the user was transitioning into polearms. Figure 4 depicts some of the standard heights for the staff with which I've worked. Anything at waist and shoulder height tends to fall into the category of such European wooden training weapons as the waster or Japanese bokken. Because of the ease of mobility, these are best used with the respective sword techniques of their country of origin rather than staff techniques per se. The techniques within this book are easily adaptable to anything from head height to 24 inches above it. Any length above this requires a different method of handing, which I will only touch on in this text.

THICKNESS

As a rule of thumb, the thickness of a staff should be determined by your ability to secure a grip as the fingers close around the staff. The structural composition and associated strength of the particular type of wood will determine the diameter size and how much flex you want for the weapon.

TYPES OF WOOD

The most common types of wood associated with the staff are oak, hazel, ash, hawthorn, and wax wood (a white wood from China that has been used for centuries for staffs and polearms). I prefer wax wood, and the staffs illustrated throughout this text are made from it. It is available through most martial art suppliers and is very popular among forms competitors. Today you have the option of buying finished staffs or kiln-dried lumber from which to make your own.

It is generally believed that the best staffs are

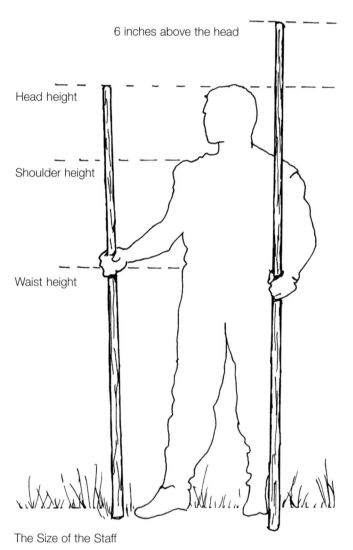

6 inches above the head

Head height

Shoulder height

Waist height

The Size of the Staff

FIGURE 4

made from whole saplings rather than branches of large trees. Saplings produce a tough, flexible staff in a varying range of sizes, which can absorb a lot of punishment without splintering. Hazel and ash saplings make light, flexible staffs, but ash has a tendency to flake and split. Hawthorn and oak are probably the toughest and most durable staff material, but they tend to be a bit rigid. As I said, I prefer wax wood.

If you want to be a traditionalist, you can make your own staff. A point to remember is that if you cut a sapling in the spring or summer, when the trees are full of sap, it will warp as it dries out. The best time to cut a sapling is in the winter. The sapling should be cut about 1 inch from the ground or just above the root ball. The freshly cut sapling should be stored in a dry shelter for about three months before stripping off the bark. A sharp knife or wood rasp may be used to remove the bark. Once the bark is removed, sand the staff smooth with coarse to fine grades of sandpaper. A few coats of light oil will help keep the moisture out of the wood.

Green bamboo of approximately 1–2 inch diameter may also be used; however, these dry out over time and may split. Covering the bamboo with duct tape immediately after cutting may help prevent this. Prior to working with staffs of green bamboo, you should sand and smooth the bamboo joints to prevent hand injury. Most bamboo tends to be a bit light; therefore, it is reasonably safe material for controlled sparring.

SECTIONS

Any serious student of the staff will eventually run across the term *quarterstaff* in his studies. The term is exclusively English, and its origin may be medieval. There are several theories about what it means, but it is generally accepted that it refers to the position of the hands on the weapon. In other words, the staff is divided into four quarters. Between 1870 and 1898 the use of the quarterstaff evolved into a form of fencing not unlike that of Japanese kendo. The Victorian manuals of this period illustrate the staff being divided into four sections identified by alphabetical points running from the tip to the heel of the weapon. Depicted in Figure 5A is *my* interpretation of this method, which is used to describe the hand positions as they are shifted along the staff for attack and defense (Figure 5B).

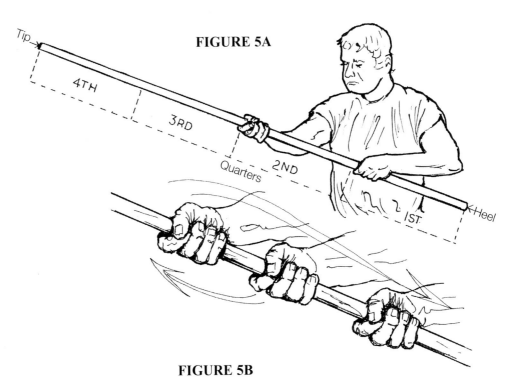

FIGURE 5A

FIGURE 5B

HAND POSITIONS

There are five basic hand positions that can be used, depending on the martial art or style of use for the weapon. In this book, I will address all of them within the context of moving the hands along the staff using a variety of attack and defensive techniques. I will refer to Figure 5A from time to time in describing various techniques. Throughout this manual I assume a right-handed user.

Quarterstaff Grip (Mixed Grip)

This grip is described in some of the Victorian quarterstaff (1850–1898) fencing manuals. It involves placing the lead hand in the forward portion of the second quarter of the staff, with the fingers to the left. The rear hand is placed in the forward portion of the first quarter of the staff, with the fingers to the right. This position allows the combatant to fight initially at long ranges and to rapidly shift the hands to the center of the staff to accommodate close-quarter work. Powerful long or short strikes can be delivered with a push-pull action of the hands. Figure 6A depicts this grip.

Overhand Grip

My sifu referred to this as the double-handed grip, where the fingers face down (Figure 6B). It is normally situated in the middle of the staff with one hand in the middle third quarter and the other in the middle second quarter of the staff. This grip is usually favored for close-quarter and levering work. This grip is particularly effective for blocking and pushing techniques.

Mixed Middle Grip

Often seen in forms competition, this grip facilitates rapid, circular, flourishing attacks, where the staff makes a series of vertical spins to block and strike. The lead hand is in the rear of the third quarter, while the rear hand rests in the first part of the second quarter (Figure 7). This grip is best used in conjunction with a small staff from 5–6 feet long. The overhand grip may also be used in this position.

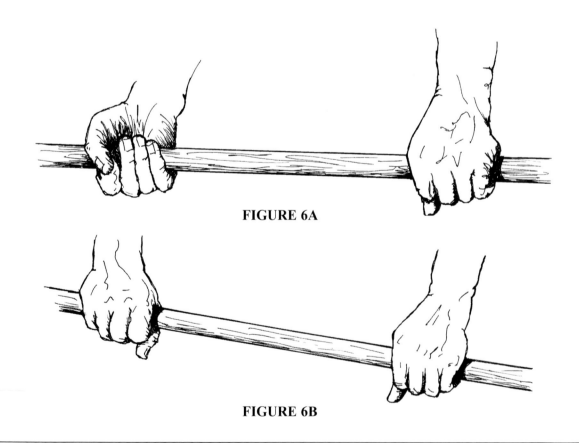

FIGURE 6A

FIGURE 6B

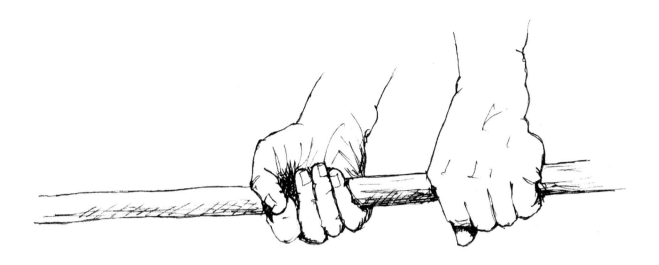

FIGURE 7

Long Grip

This grip allows the staff to be employed at long range with techniques similar to those used with the Renaissance longsword and polearms. It facilitates the long- and medium-range engagements with both long and short strikes. While the impact of most strikes developed with the long grip is not as power-ful as that generated by using the overhand and mixed grips, you can deliver much faster long-range thrusts without closing with an opponent. Place the lead hand in the middle of the second quarter and the rear hand about 1 inch from the heel of the staff (Figure 8).

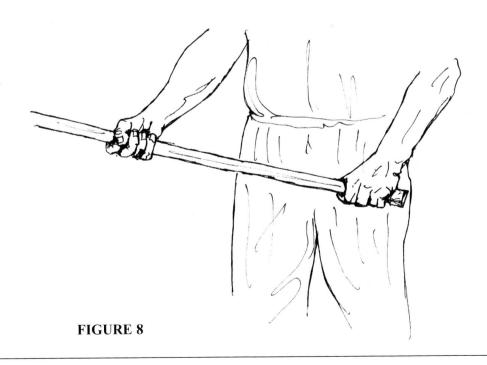

FIGURE 8

Reverse Grip

This grip appears in several Renaissance fight books—the mixed or overhand grip is used with the lead hand in a fingers-up position on the heel and the rear hand in the middle of the second quarter (Figure 9). It is primarily used for ascending strikes or lever techniques against an opponent's legs. Since a major portion of the staff is behind the user, its effectiveness is situation dependent (an issue not addressed in this book).

FIGURE 9

CHAPTER 2
FIGHTING STANCE

The staff grips directly relate to the fighting stance that you may assume before, during, and after an engagement. You might say they are one and the same. Assuming a fighting stance involves determining which hand and which leg should be forward or closer to the opponent. While there are many ideas about the handedness and superiority of one stance over another, the truth rests with being able to move the staff into position to take advantage of an opening. It involves being able to fight with the staff along either the left or right side of the body. Before going into this aspect, let's take a look at the major fighting stances (guards) that have been handed down to us from both European and Asian cultures. Any study of history, whether Asian or European, will reveal three common guards or fighting stances that can be used with the grips addressed earlier.

MIDDLE GUARD

This stance originated with the Elizabethan teacher George Silver. It uses a mixed grip that is very similar to the long grip except that the rear hand is placed about 12–18 inches from the heel of the staff. The advantage of this guard/grip is that it allows you to adjust your grip and move your hands rapidly over any portion of the staff in order to work a variety of ranges. It also provides protection from attack at any level. In 1638 Miyamoto Musashi spoke very highly of this type of guard being suited to most circumstances:

> "Whatever guard position you assume, do not think of taking a position, instead think of being ready to strike. . . . The middle-level guard position is fundamental. In fact, the middle-guard position is the original guard."

In *The Book of Five Rings,* Musashi also recommended varying the position of the weapon by pointing it directly at the opponent's face. He saw this as a means of keeping an opponent at a given distance by varying angles horizontally and vertically. The middle-guard stance can be used on either side of the body with either leg or hand forward. It is particularly useful in delivering thrusts.

Middle Guard

The range of position for this guard

Either the right or left hand or leg can be forward.

FIGURE 10

HIGH GUARD

The advantage of this guard is that it puts you into position to deliver powerful descending strikes without having to move into position, as when using the middle guard. The disadvantage is that it exposes the lower body to attack. You should think of this particular guard as being assumed in conjunction with movement that takes advantage of a target of opportunity. As with the middle guard, either hand or leg can be forward, depending on which side of the body the staff is held.

High Guard

This is the range of position for this guard.

Either the right or left hand or leg can be forward.

FIGURE 11

Low Guard

This is the range of position for this guard.

Either the right or left hand or leg can be forward.

FIGURE 12

LOW GUARD

This guard is very effective for delivering powerful ascending strikes into an opponent's lower body. While it provides excellent protection for your legs, it exposes the upper body to attack (Figure 12).

NOTE: While our illustrations show these guards with a modified mixed middle grip, they can also be used effectively with the long grip for medium-range engagements.

USING THE ENTIRE STAFF

Those three are the primary stances/guards and associated grips used in this text. But remember, the entire staff should be used as opportunities present themselves in an engagement. Rather than attempting to fight with only one specific stance or grip, you use a variety of positions and grips along the staff to gain the advantage of time, distance, and position. For example, if during the fight your opponent closes, you shift to the quarterstaff grip to gain the advantage of close-quarter pinning and levering.

Another example: when an opponent attacks and then moves out of range, you shift to the long grip to engage him as he moves away. Before I get too deep into this, let's review some of the conceptual "language" used when talking about a fighting staff.

THE CONCEPT OF INSIDE AND OUTSIDE THE BOX

The idea of using the entire staff is not new. Many of the Renaissance masters alluded to this when describing which hand and leg should be forward with specific stances. Although they differed somewhat in terms and applications, both Asian and Western instructors agreed that fighting with the staff should be done from both sides of the body with either the left or right leg forward.

Before progressing further, it is important to understand the term "inside and outside the box." This is a historical fencing concept that addresses your position in relation to the stance and position of the weapon of your opponent. In Figure 13 you face an opponent from a position inside the box. In this frontal position, you are subject to attack or immediate counterattack. Note that the opponent is armed with two weapons, which makes this situation particularly dangerous for you because he is able to attack from different angles in the box. Now, don't get the idea you can't attack in this area. Just be aware that it is dangerous.

Inside

FIGURE 13

Figure 14 depicts the same opponent as seen from outside the box. This is the preferred place to be when attacking, as your opponent must turn toward you to attack. Keep in mind that these figures depict rather extreme examples and that during the course of an engagement you will probably be faced with slightly different views as the opponent moves. Remember that these may well be fleeting glimpses of specific target areas.

Now let's look at another aspect of this concept. When you are facing an opponent using a two-handed sword or another staff, the position of the lead

Outside

FIGURE 14

leg and hand becomes important. Because the staff is used with two hands and the weapon crosses the body, you might say that the staff connects both sides of you and your opponent. In Figure 15 you can see the position of your opponent armed with a staff weapon. He is in a high guard, or quarterstaff, stance with his right leg and hand forward. Note that

he is in position to block or counterattack any strike made by the front or rear portions of the staff illustrated in position A. Some teachers refer to this side of the opponent as being "closed," with the only target opportunity being the lead hand or leg. Note that the majority of the target opportunities are to the opponent's left side, or inside.

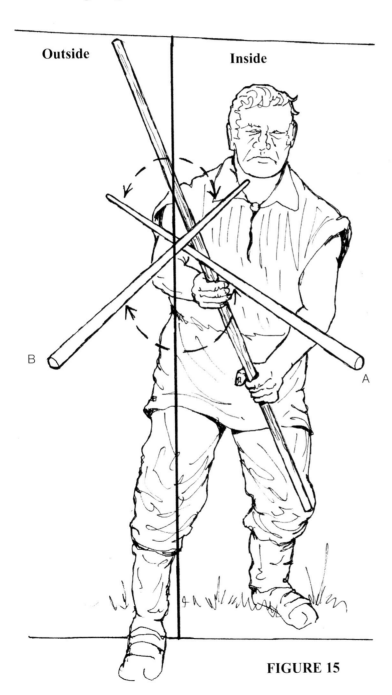

Outside **Inside**

B

A

FIGURE 15

"Always standing crosse with your enemie, I meanie, if his right hand and foote be foremost, let yours be so likewise, and if his left hand and foote be foremost, then make you your change and crosse with him also. . . . Now, if your enemie doth assault you upon the contraie side, you must change both your foote and hand to crosse with him, as before."
—Joseph Swetnam, 1617

With this statement Swetnam lays down one of the primary principles for staff fighting against a similar weapon. Figure 15 illustrates his point: staff drawing B crosses over into the opponent's inside. Basically, you are taking up the same stance or position as the opponent. The bottom line: you will have to change stances and hand positions during an engagement to gain the advantage. This leads to my next point and your first training exercise.

CHAPTER 3
ASPECTS OF HAND AND POSITION CHANGE

There are many different ways to effect a hand change to give you inside position. You can also move to a different grip to gain advantage. For now you are only concerned with the movement from a middle or quarterstaff guard from one side to another.

TRAINING OBJECTIVE 1

Task: Effect a hand change from a stance with the right leg forward to a stance with the left leg forward.

Condition: Given a staff and training area sufficient to accommodate 360-degree movement and overhead strikes with the weapon.

Standard:

Action 1: Let's start off by assuming middle guard with the right leg and hand forward, as seen in Figure 15. Slide the left hand forward about 6 inches (Figure 16). This should place your hand in the middle point of balance for the weapon.

Action 2: As soon as the left hand is in place, immediately release the right

hand and place it approximately 6 inches below the left hand, which will now become the lead hand. Simultaneously with the hand movement, step forward with the left leg, passing the right leg into a left-leg-lead position, as seen in Figures 17 and 18. As the left leg goes forward, swing the heel of the staff over to your right side and assume the stance depicted in Figures 19 and 20.

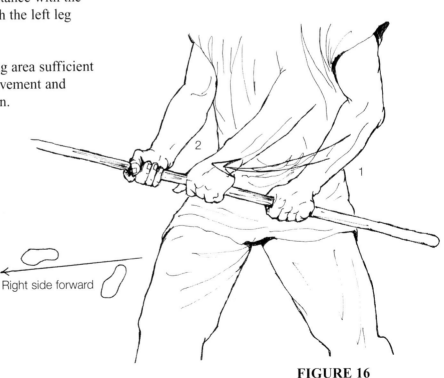

Right side forward

FIGURE 16

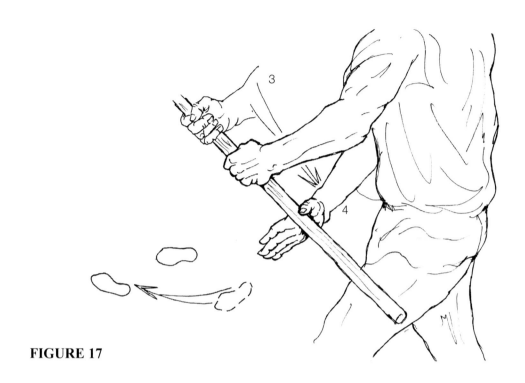

FIGURE 17

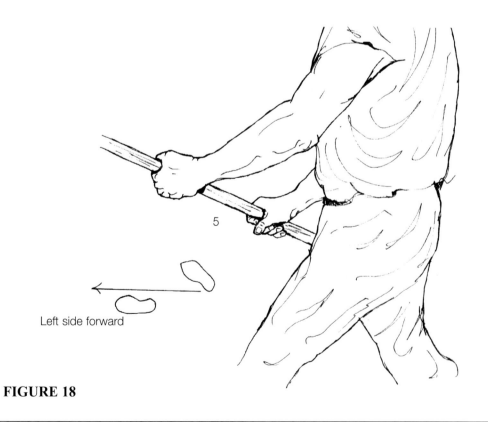

Left side forward

FIGURE 18

Action 3: As soon as you are in the left-leg-leading position, immediately reverse Actions 1 and 2 by stepping back with the left leg. This completes a full repetition.

Action 4: Execute approximately 10–15 repetitions (Actions 1–3) until you are comfortable with the hand change. If possible get in front of a mirror and experiment with this while holding the staff first vertically and then horizontally against the body. Note how moving the staff vertically

can expose you to potential attack. The point is that when executing this hand change, you should attempt to keep the staff as close as possible to the middle-guard position. It may be necessary to slide the hand back a bit toward the heel of the staff to accomplish this.

Action 5 (Hand-Change Drill): Post yourself in front of a training partner, who is also armed with a staff. Assume the middle guard position discussed in Action 1 and extend your arms, holding the staff horizontally. Adjust your position with your partner so that the tips of the staffs are approximately 2 inches apart (almost touching). Now move the arms back to the flexed position of the original stance. You are now out of range of each other's strikes, which is a requirement for this next drill.

Both partners assume a right-leg-forward position. On the command "Begin!" your partner will execute a hand change to a left-leg-for-ward position. As soon as you sense his movement to change the hand position, as seen in Figure 19, move your staff from position A to B, illustrated in Figure 20. Repeat this action about 10 to 15 times.

Pay particular attention to the visual movement indicators illustrated by positions 1 through 3 in Figure 19. Note how the staff moves to clear the heel of the weapon to swing over to the opposite side. Look for the hand release seen in position 3. Later you will find that an opportune time to attack an opponent is

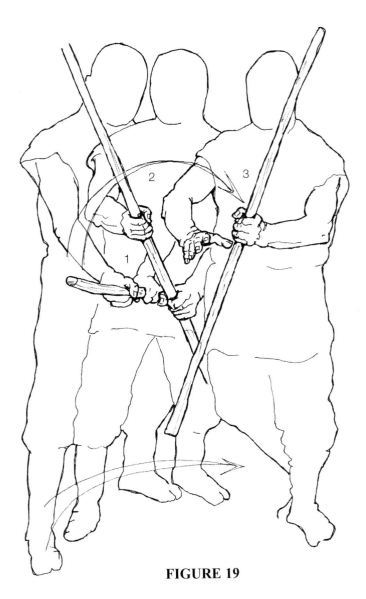

FIGURE 19

during this hand change. As you work through this drill with your partner, look for attack openings similar to the one seen in Figure 21.

NOTE: The primary reason I included the discussion and concept for Figures 15–21 in this text is because this approach is commonly used today (as in the past) by a number of very qualified and highly professional scholars of the staff. This is a fencing concept that was grounded in the use of the sword and should apply only to those occasions when you grip the staff with the rear hand on the heel similar to the long-grip stance we referred to earlier. Like the Elizabethan teacher Joseph Swetnam, many teachers of that time saw the staff as a transition to the polearms of that period, which emphasized engagements at range, and part of a system that supported a transition into battlefield formations and a variety of other pole weapons.

"When one would give you a swinging blow, right-hander to right-hander. If you have the croix in front, you can step forward with your left foot, receiving his blow, picking it up with the queue of your axe and in a single movement bear downward to make his axe fall to the ground."
—Unknown author of *Le Jeu de la Hache*,
a 15th-century treatise on
the use of the poleaxe

That said, for me, there is no inside and outside the box as it applies to the staff, other than that depicted in Figures 13 and 14. When you face an

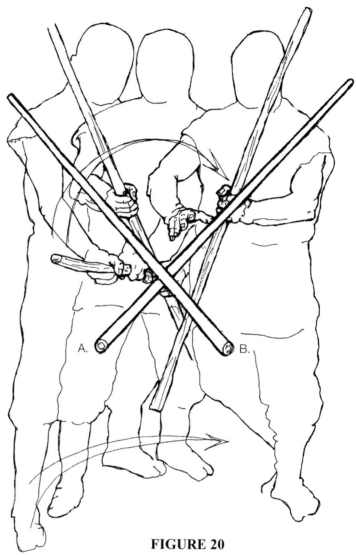

FIGURE 20

opponent armed with a staff, you should always think of yourself as inside the box, regardless of whether you cross his staff with yours or not. I base this on the rationale that regardless of which leg or hand is forward, you can be hit with both ends of the opponent's weapons. When you consider some of the Asian attack methods that use pulling and cross-arm techniques, it is clear that it is not always necessary to effect a hand or leg change. I think the hand change has value as a training vehicle, and it does permit opportunities when you catch your opponent in the middle of

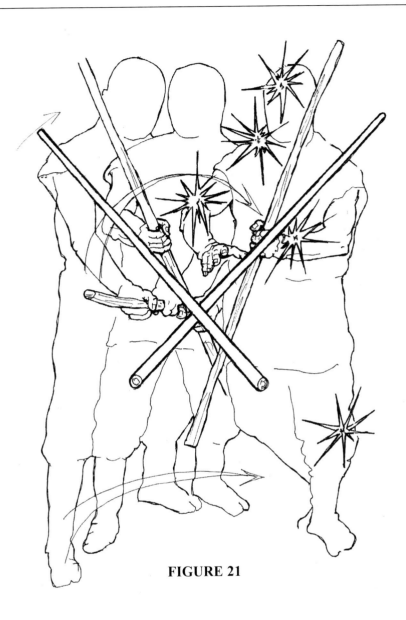

FIGURE 21

making such a change. My comments here are not intended to discredit the methods or teachers that promote this approach, but rather to give the reader another approach to experiment with the application. Study the hand change and practice it regularly, but do not consider it more than a conceptual tool to gain an advantage.

CHAPTER 4
ASPECTS OF STAFF FOOTWORK

In Figures 22 through 27, you will find a series of footwork sets that cover the basic footwork associated with most martial arts weaponry. These sets are a modification derived from the Spanish System of Fence detailed in Girard Thibault's 1610 text *Academy of the Sword.* You will also see similar footwork patterns in the Filipino martial arts as well. You might say these are solid, basic practice patterns, which can be used equally well for both attack and defense, regardless of the weapon being used. Take a moment to review and become familiar with them.

Step Forward and Backward Set
Begin with the right leg in a forward fighting stance:

- Step forward with the right leg and then bring the left leg up to assume the same fighting stance.
- Immediately step back with the left foot and then bring the right leg back to assume the fighting stance.

Use: This foot movement is also identified as an advancing step. This movement is used in a cautionary manner to cover short distances as you move into striking range of an opponent.

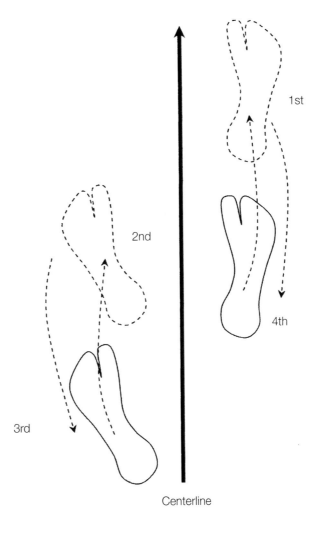

Centerline

FIGURE 22

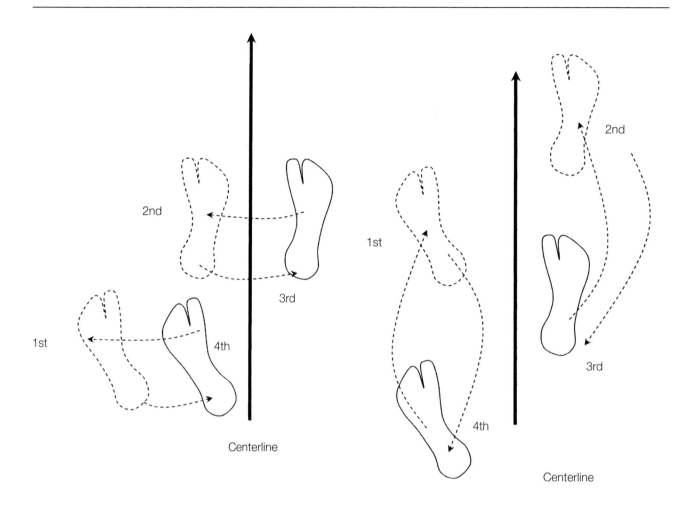

FIGURE 23

FIGURE 24

Step Left and Step Right Set
Begin with the right leg in a forward fighting stance:

- Step left with the left leg and then bring the right leg across the centerline to the fighting stance.
- Immediately step right with the right foot back astride the centerline and then step right with the left leg to the original fighting stance.

Use: This foot movement is used to move into an advantageous attack position or to avoid an incoming attack.

Pass Forward and Back Set
Begin with the right leg in a forward fighting stance:

- Step forward with the left leg passing the right and stopping in a fighting stance with the left leg forward. Immediately step forward with the right leg passing the left and stopping in the original fighting stance.
- Immediately step backward with the right leg passing the right and stopping in the original fighting stance.

Use: This foot movement is used to cover a lot of space during offense or defense.

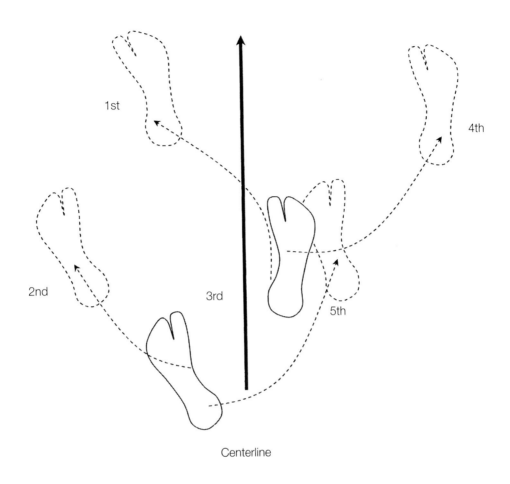

1st

4th

2nd

3rd

5th

Centerline

FIGURE 25

Traverse Forward Left and Right Set
Begin with the right leg in a forward fighting stance:

- Step forward across the centerline with the right leg and then follow with the left leg passing into the fighting stance. Immediately reverse the process and move back astride the centerline in a fighting stance.

- Step forward to the right with the right leg. Immediately follow with the left leg into the original fighting stance. Move back astride the centerline.

Use: This foot movement is used for attacking forward or evading an opponent's attack.

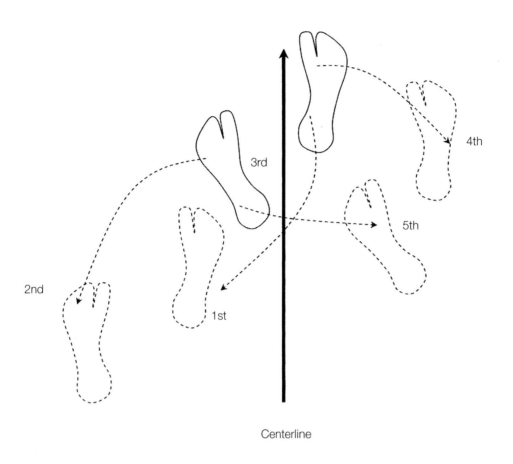

FIGURE 26

Traverse Backward Left and Right Set
Begin with the right leg in a forward fighting stance:

- Step backward and left across the centerline with the right leg and then follow with the left leg passing into the fighting stance. Immediately reverse the process and move back astride the centerline in a fighting stance.

- Step backward to the right with the right leg. Immediately follow with the left leg into the original fighting stance. Move back astride the centerline.

Use: This foot movement is used for attacking forward or evading an opponent's attack.

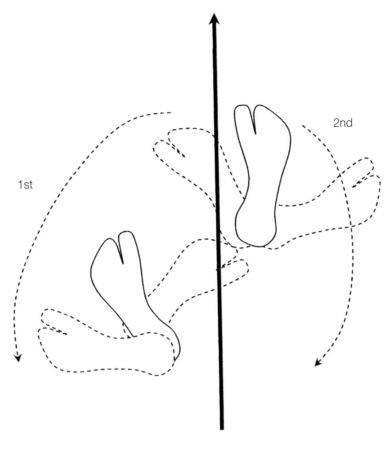

Centerline

FIGURE 27

Angle Left and Right Set
Begin with the right leg in a forward fighting stance:

- While staying astride the centerline and rotating on both heels, face the left. Immediately return to the original position.

- Repeat this rotating process while turning to face the right.

Use: This foot movement is used for avoiding incoming attacks without major foot movement.

TRAINING OBJECTIVE 2

Task: Develop a working knowledge of the foot-work pattern sets and the guard positions that will be used with the staff.

Conditions:

Condition 1: You need a staff and sufficient training area to accommodate 360-degree movement, overhead strikes, and a 20-foot distance.

Condition 2: Lay out a 15-foot line on the floor with good commercially available masking tape. If you are outside, you may want to use line marker dust. The purpose of this line is to establish a centerline to which to relate the footwork sets. Take up a position in a middle guard at one end and astride the centerline.

Standard:

Action 1: Execute a step forward and assume a high guard (Figure 28).

FIGURE 28

Step Forward and Step Backward Footwork Set with Movements Through Middle to High to Low Guards

Action 1
- Assume Middle Guard
- Step Forward to High Guard

Action 2
- From High Guard Position
- Step Backward to Low Guard

Action 2: As soon as the high guard is reached, immediately execute a step backward and assume a low guard (Figure 28).

Action 3: Move back into the middle guard and repeat the exercise 10 to 15 times until you are comfortable with the actions.

Action 5: Execute the Step Left and Step Right Set, moving to the middle, high, and low guards as in Actions 1 and 2.

Action 6: Execute the Pass Forward and Back Set, moving to the middle, high, and low guards as in previous actions.

Action 7: Execute the Traverse Forward and Right Set, moving to the middle, high, and low guards as in previous actions.

Action 8: Execute the Traverse Backward Left and Right Set, moving to the middle, high, and low guards as in previous actions.

Action 9: Execute Angle Left and Right Set, moving to the middle, high, and low guards as in previous actions.

CHAPTER 5
ASPECTS OF THE STRIKE

"The sword paints in lines, while a knife makes a cross; but the staff illustrates a circle."
—Dwight C. McLemore

This drawing is a form of Zen calligraphy called enso, or that which is concerned with the drawing of a circle as a spiritual ritual that leads toward enlightenment. The Zen masters loved to draw circles and usually accompanied them with a poem or question. The themes of these were as varied as the many aspects of Buddhism itself. The circle can be drawn left to right or right to left, depending on whether the illustrator is concerned with practicing the hard or easy way—i.e., basically, going with or against the flow of things. The staff is a weapon that attacks and defends with some form of circular motion. The message of the staff and its use is not unlike this Zen concept: moving left or right and revealing openings of success the easy or the hard way. The enso I drew was drawn first in one direction and then the other. The Chinese calligraphic symbol is that of the stick or staff. Think about this as you read the rest of this manual.

Enso of the Staff

In the West the dragon is viewed as an evil, fearsome beast. In Asia this mythical creature represents a totally positive force. Dragons are often associated with weather conditions, mountains, and water. While their wings are not apparent, they do possess the ability to fly. The dragon has come to symbolize the Chinese culture and is frequently represented in much of China's art, literature, and music.

The dragon is known to be the symbol of creative power. Because of their association with nature, I have always thought that dragons would probably have an affinity for the staff since it is nothing but a tree. Back in the late 1990s when my school was operational, I created the drawing seen here to grace a certificate of completion for the staff curriculum I taught. It more or less sums up the creative power and limitless potential of this very basic weapon. I've also included a bit of prose that I wrote back in 1980 to my children about the Asian dragon. May the spirit of the dragon ride your staff as you conduct your training.

To Lea Anne and Alicia Marie:

Dragons

To me dragons are wonderful things, mischievous beings of a nether world that flow back and forth between our time and theirs.

They are personable beings, who for all their fierce appearance seem to reserve their flames for those who do not believe.

My fascination with them is hard to explain—perhaps not unlike a small child's interest in some frog or lizard that has crossed the path.

The favor of dragons is often elusive, even as the minnow avoids the tiny hand that seeks to touch him in a crystal pool.

Dragons are dreams and inspiration that often pull one out of bed in the middle of the night to make some note or put a finishing touch on a piece of art.

They represent the hope, drive, and strength to always look forward to something no matter how unattainable.

My children, *my dragons*, are with me now. Believe in them; your father always did.

The story of the staff is one of strikes, blocks, and deflection. It is about realizing the full potential of the weapon by working its entire length, capitalizing on the needs of the situation and a variety of target opportunities. Sorry if that came across as some philosophical bull, but I think it is pretty accurate for what you need to do with the staff. Foremost, you should think of the staff conceptually as a weapon of motion, and this motion is contained in half circles that swing back and forth within a range of approximately 180 degrees, depending on your body position and the technique being applied. There are one horizontal circle and one vertical circle, as depicted in Figures 29 and 30, respectively. The vertical circles are not limited to just the sides of the body but can cross in front, as depicted in Figure 31, where they take on the aspects of strikes or deflection methods.

High

Middle

Low

FIGURE 29

FIGURE 30

Opponent

FIGURE 31

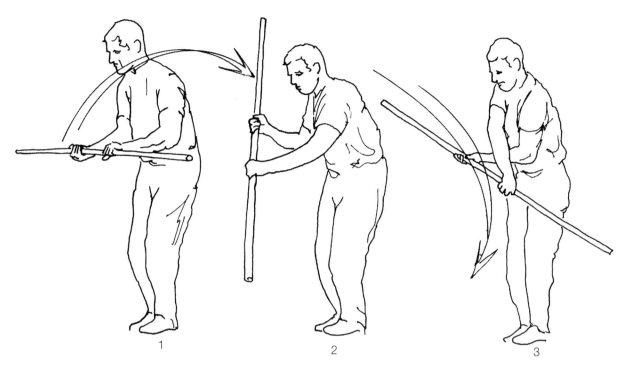

1　　2　　3

FIGURE 32

Let's take a moment to get a feel for this conceptual aspect through the use of a pattern of figure-eight swings, often referred to as a flourish.

TRAINING OBJECTIVE 3

Task: To acquire a feel for the conceptual aspect of the circular motions the staff makes during attack and defense. Please note that this *is not a fighting technique*, but rather an exercise designed to make you familiar with the circular-motion capability of the staff.

Condition: You must have a staff and sufficient training to accommodate 360-degree movement and overhead strikes.

Standard:

Action 1: Take up a position with the feet together (as in illustration 1 of Figure 32) and the knees slightly bent. Assume a mixed grip with the fingers up on the right hand and down on the left.

Action 2: Begin by bringing the right hand over to the left, as seen in illustrations 2 and 3 of Figure 32.

4   5   6

FIGURE 33

Action 3: As the tip of the staff arcs over in Action 2, pull the right hand back to the direction of the starting position while pushing with the left hand to move the heel up and over, as seen in illustrations 4–6 of Figure 33.

7   8   9

FIGURE 34

Action 4: As Action 3 is completed, swing the tip back over to the left and repeat Action 2 again. Check out illustrations 7–9 of Figure 34 to see this process.

Action 5: Repeat this figure-eight pattern 10 to 15 times directly to the front in a circular flowing motion. Pay particular attention to how the staff can be moved from the high- to low-line areas. Note how the staff can strike with a pushing action and deflect with a pulling action. Try bending the knees to change the horizontal plane and then alternate dropping each leg back, noting how the leading leg affects this motion.

Action 6: This time repeat Action 6 while twisting your trunk to the left and right, as seen earlier in Figure 30.

NOTE: As I said earlier, this is simply an exercise. It is really good to warm up and loosen the hands and wrists in preparation for striking exercises. You might consider changing to other types of grip and observe how the staff is affected.

You should think of the staff as a weapon of motion. It has a rhythm that follows a beat, sounding like "woosh, boom, woosh" or even "boom-ta-boom" as it circles to strike with either end. Movements should flow from one into another.

STRIKING TECHNIQUES

The staff is often defined as an impact weapon. In other words, it relies on the force of a given blow, as opposed to cutting action associated with knives and swords. It breaks bones and crushes muscle tissue and ligaments. There is almost an immediate reaction from an opponent on receiving an effective strike to the head or joint. On most other body parts, the blunt-force trauma associated with the strike can produce instant shock and internal bleeding. On a less-lethal note, many striking techniques can be delivered to disable rather than kill an opponent.

DIRECTIONAL DELIVERY

Staff strikes can be delivered with either the heel

or tip of the staff leading. Depending on the target impact, strikes can be made using any of the quarters addressed earlier. Strikes are normally identified by three general types: descending, horizontal, and ascending. These strikes are generically associated with eight areas on an opponent.

The above is part of the "language" used to train students in proper targeting techniques. Historically, they have been referred to as the *angles of attack* and can be found in both Eastern and Western martial arts under a variety of names. Figure 35 illustrates a contemporary rendition of these target areas seen as you face a hypothetical opponent armed with a staff. These angles are used throughout this manual. For example, "Step to the left, avoiding his thrust and deliver an *Angle 1* strike to the left side of your opponent's head."

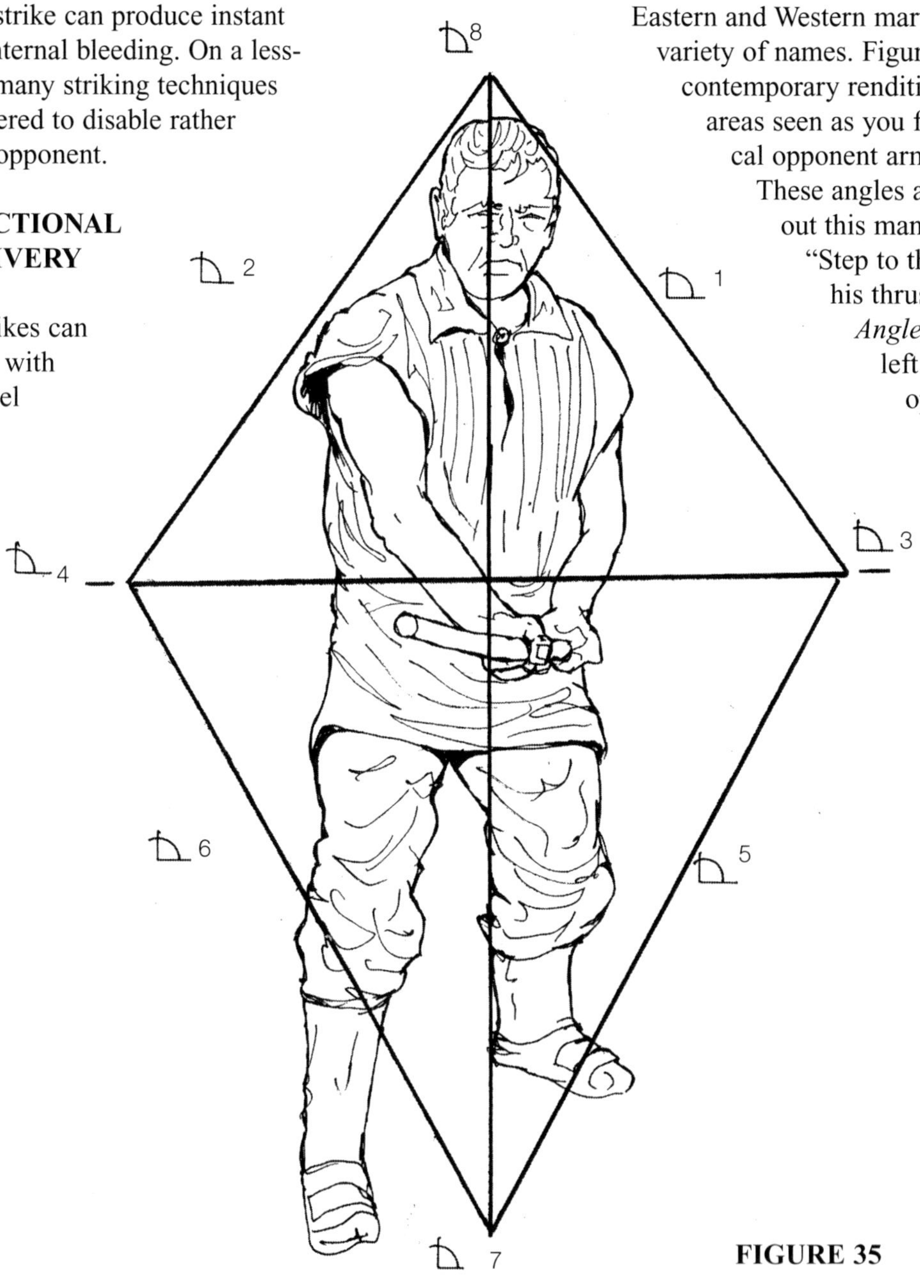

FIGURE 35

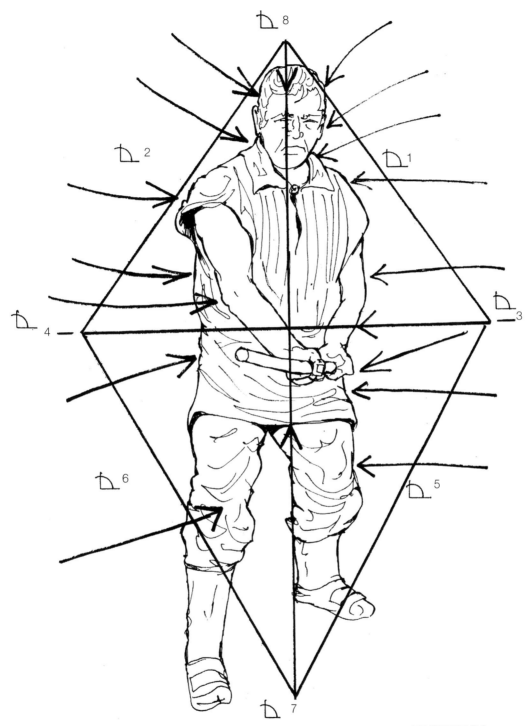

FIGURE 36

Figure 36 depicts some of the potential targets in the respective angle areas. Note that Angles 1, 2, 5, and 6 have the potential for delivering descending, ascending, and horizontal strikes using either end of the staff. Naturally, this depends on the situation and position.

FIGURE 37

TYPES OF STRIKES

The long strike and the short strike are the two primary types of strikes that can be delivered against targets within the angles just discussed, but I have included two others in this book: the one-two strike and the cross-body strike. Both the long and short strike are executed with the push-pull action illustrated in Figure 37.

Long Strike
Long strikes are usually delivered by either raising or lowering the staff into position to strike, with either the tip or heel of the weapon. Figure 38 depicts a long strike being delivered into the Angle 1 area.

FIGURE 38

The action involves first moving the tip of the staff up over the head or right shoulder. The staff is pulled down with the lead hand pushing and the rear hand pulling forcefully in an arc that passes the heel of the staff across the abdomen. As the upper quarter of the staff descends, there is a slight twisting of the hands, not unlike wringing water from a damp towel. The far left illustration in Figure 37 depicts the direction each hand takes during this motion. Note in the footwork diagrams in Figure 38 how

there is a downward torque of the hips that turns the torso slightly into the opponent in the direction of the strike and adds great power to the strike.

In Figure 39 we have a view of our opponent as we face him with the right hand and leg in the forward position. In the next series of illustrations you will explore the aspects of the various long strikes into specific target angle areas. In these drawings I use the floating staff to depict the major target areas that can be acquired for each area.

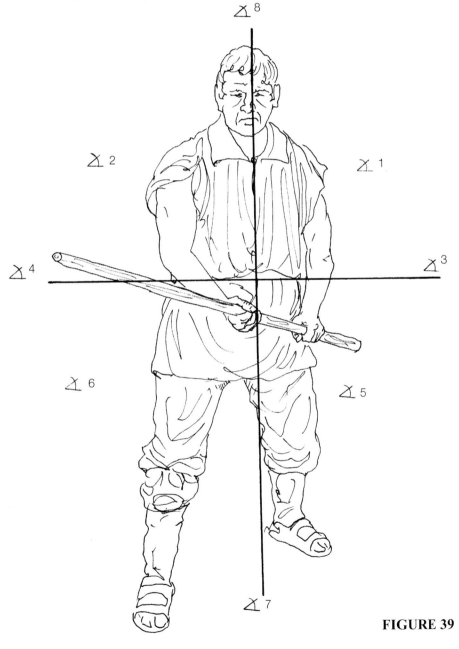

FIGURE 39

Angle Area 1: Take a close look at Figure 40. Notice that these attacks are delivered with the tip of the staff using the wringing action mentioned earlier. It is also important to note that when you are in a position with the left leg and hand forward, as after a changeover, you will be delivering the strikes into Angle Area 2.

Angle Area 2: Figure 41 depicts the long strike into Angle Area 2 impacting with the heel of the staff. The position of the hands and arms here makes it difficult to accomplish the same wringing action used earlier, the result being that you have to rely more on the rotation of the hips and push-pull action to increase the force of the impact. Figure 42 depicts this descending strike on the opponent.

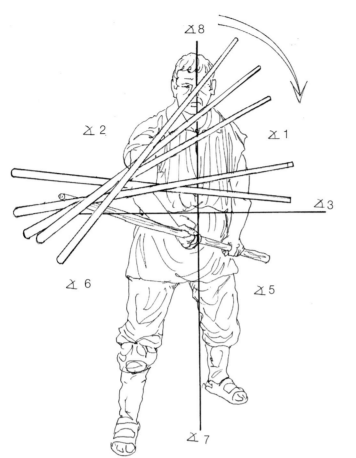

FIGURE 40

FIGURE 41

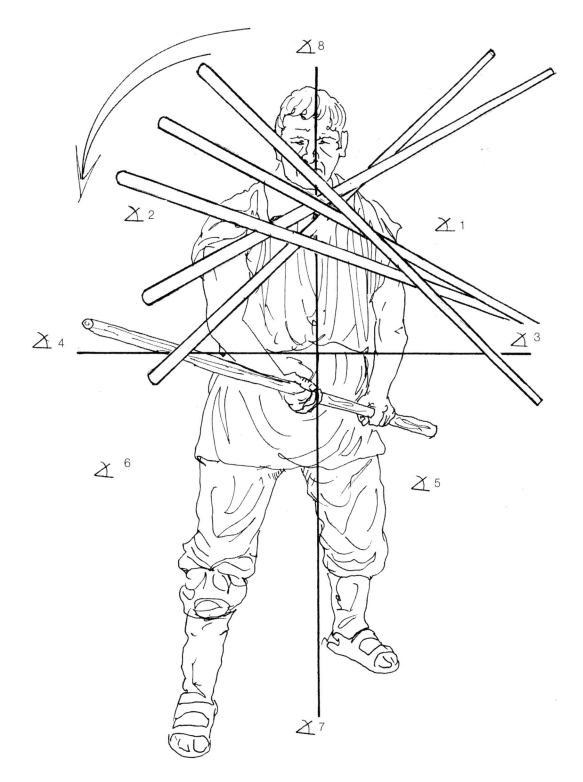

FIGURE 42

One-Two Strike

A common striking technique involves following a strike into Angle Area 1 with an immediate strike with the heel of the staff into Angle Area 2. These combinations of high-line strikes are particularly effective when an opponent blocks your first strike. When practicing this, you should vary the specific targets. For example, the first strike is an Angle 1 to the neck followed immediately by an Angle 2 to the elbow.

Angle Areas 3 and 4: Figure 43 depicts the horizontal attacks into Angle Areas 3 and 4. Note how the hands have shifted to the center of the staff to facilitate close-quarter strikes to an opponent's elbows, hips, and hands. For both these strikes, the staff is pulled close to your torso with the motion swinging across the hip line. When possible, a slight flexing of the legs is needed to really put the hip action into these strikes. Figure 44 presents a view of angle areas.

FIGURE 43

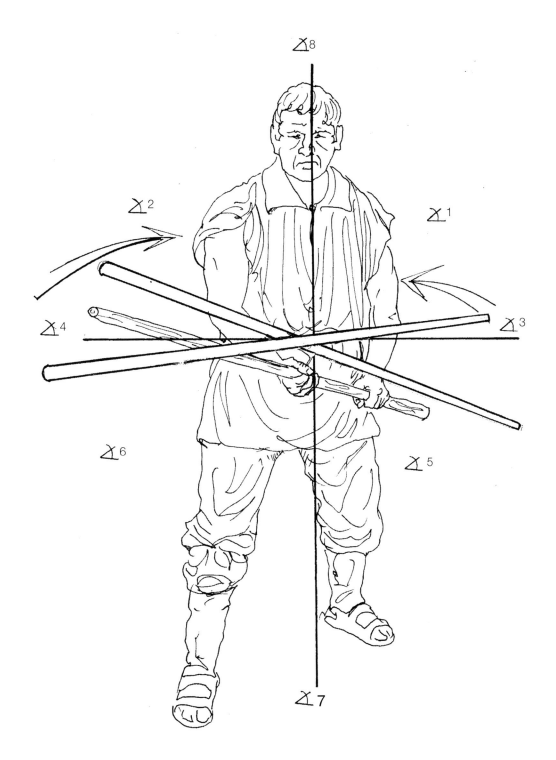

FIGURE 44

FIGURE 45

Angle Area 5: In Figure 45 you see the first ascending strike targeting the opponent's knee, hip, rear hand, and elbow. These strikes can be accomplished at medium range with the hands positioned as depicted earlier in Figure 10 for the middle guard. A simple shift of the hands to the middle of the staff in quarters 2 and 3 will facilitate its use for close range, similar to Angle Areas 3 and 4. This strike is executed with a strong push-pull action of the arms and shoulder, with a slight downward compression or dip of the hips. In Figure 45 note how the feet slide forward into the opponent with a turn that slams the tip of the staff into the target area at an acute angle. Figure 46 depicts this angle.

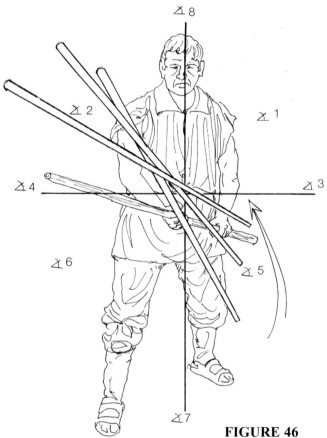

FIGURE 46

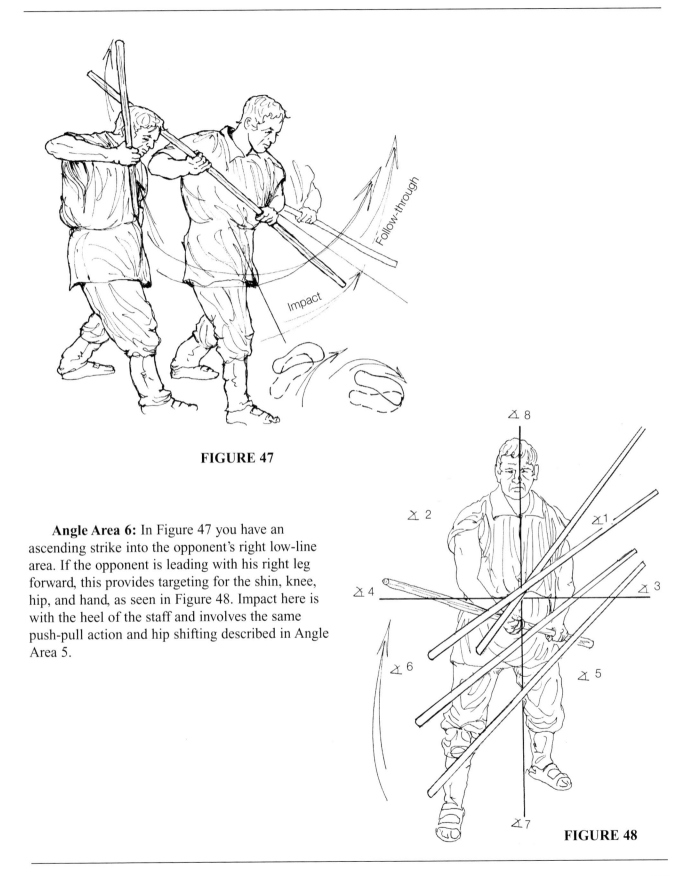

FIGURE 47

FIGURE 48

Angle Area 6: In Figure 47 you have an ascending strike into the opponent's right low-line area. If the opponent is leading with his right leg forward, this provides targeting for the shin, knee, hip, and hand, as seen in Figure 48. Impact here is with the heel of the staff and involves the same push-pull action and hip shifting described in Angle Area 5.

Angle Areas 7 and 8: Figure 49 depicts the third ascending strike, which drives the tip of the staff into the groin area of an opponent. In addition to the push-pull action described in the proceeding angle areas, there is a lifting action with the shoulders as you step into the opponent. Figure 50 presents a descending strike into Angle Area 8. Step into the opponent from left to right and driving the heel of the staff down onto his head will accomplish this. During the execution of this action, it may be necessary to rise up onto the balls of the feet to gain sufficient height and force for this blow. As with Angle Areas 3 and 4, these strikes should be performed with one following the other using the same action of the horizontal one-two strike approach. Figure 51 depicts this action against the opponent.

FIGURE 49

FIGURE 50

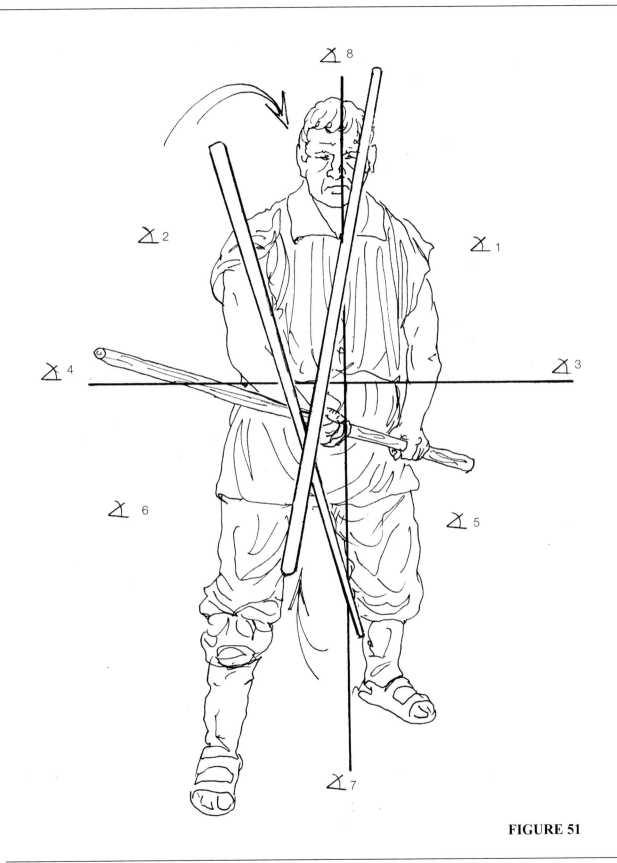

FIGURE 51

Cross-Body Strike

In Chinese staff work you will see some long strikes executed with one arm or another ending up across the body. These are not as powerful as those described earlier, but they can be quite effective for disrupting an opponent's attack or clearing his weapon prior to executing a conventional strike.

Right-Side Impact

Figure 52 illustrates the cross-body strike to the right of the centerline. It begins by executing a clearing action with the heel of the staff that follows a line similar to that of a strike into Angle Area 2. As the heel passes the centerline, the left hand pulls the heel back up and under the right arm. Simultaneously, the right hand slams the tip of the staff down into high-line targets in Angle Area 1 with a pushing action.

FIGURE 52

Left-Side Impact

Figure 53 depicts another cross-body descending strike with the tip of the staff leading. Start out with the staff in a middle guard and drop the tip of the staff down and to your left as if to disrupt a low-line attack. Continue to swing the tip up and over your left shoulder while stepping into the opponent. Violently pull the tip down into the Angle 2 target area.

FIGURE 53

The Short Strike

These cross-body strikes should be practiced both independently and as part of one continuous flow with the right- and left-side techniques being executed one after another.

Short Strike

These strikes are executed directly from a middle guard position. They are used when your opponent's action will not permit use of a long strike. The short strike is executed with a short snapping action at the end of a rapid ascending extension of the arms. Figure 54 depicts this motion. Note that the hands execute the same wringing action described in the Angle Area 1 long strike. The feel of this strike is not unlike a thrust with a rapid snap at the end. There is usually a forward slide with the feet during

FIGURE 54

the action (Figure 55). Figure 56 depicts the common target areas that the short strike can be used against to disrupt and create openings for a follow-on attack. This technique is particularly effective against the hands.

FIGURE 55

FIGURE 56

TRAINING OBJECTIVE 4

Task: Execute the staff long strikes into the eight target areas.

Condition: You must have a staff and sufficient training area to accommodate 360-degree movement and overhead strikes with the weapon. If possible, practice this exercise in front of a mirror. If one is not available, I recommend you train outside with your back to the sun so that you can use your shadow as a guide to correct technique. Another approach is to use a wall chart depicting a full-size human silhouette, similar to that shown in Figure 35. The point of this exercise is to become familiar with the delivery of long strikes at the various targets within the eight target areas discussed earlier. You are not concerned with delivering hard fast strikes initially. Just complete each action slowly and smoothly, and focus on the correct swing and footwork. Take your time and get the "feel" of the weapon.

Standard:

Action 1: Start off in a middle-guard position depicted earlier. Visualize an opponent facing you with a staff. Suddenly, he makes a short strike at your head, and you immediately sidestep to the right and forward while delivering a strike to any target with Angle 1 target areas (Figure 40). Visualize your opponent blocking the strike, which you immediately counter by stepping forward with the left leg and striking with the heel of the staff into a target within the Angle 2 target area (Figure 41). This is the one-two strike concept discussed earlier. Assume your second strike was successful and your opponent falls. Return to the middle-guard position. Repeat this process at least 10 times, putting focus on the hips and footwork. During this process, remember to execute the slight "wringing-the-towel action" of the hands. Practice this action at

slow speed before moving on to medium and finally full speed. Remember that you are fighting at medium range, and impacts are made within the fourth and first quarters of the staff, respectively.

Action 2: Visualize your opponent sliding forward into close range. Shift your right hand into the third quarter and the left into the fourth quarter, and immediately execute a strike into a target with Angle 3 target areas. Imagine your opponent blocking this first blow and you immediately following with a strike into the Angle 4 target area. Remember, you are pulling the staff tightly against your body in the general vicinity of the hips. The execution of these strikes requires you to violently shift the hip into the target while holding your arms tight to the sides, performing the push-pull action. As you push the staff from one side to the other, there should be a slight flexing of the legs, first down and then up into the direction of the strike. This puts a slightly upward angle of the strikes that can throw the opponent off balance. Study Figure 43 to understand these dynamics.

As with Action 1, practice this one-two combination at slow speed till you get the mechanics right, and then move with 10 to 15 repetitions at medium and fast speed.

Action 3: Figures 45–48 illustrate the one-two attacks into the low-line area, specifically Angles 5 and 6, respectively. Visualize your opponent stepping back into medium range and assuming a position with his left leg forward. As he moves, slide to the right outside and deliver a strike into the knee in Angle 5 target area. Your staff should swing down and up into the target impact within the fourth or third quarter of your staff. Don't forget to flex the knees slightly and turn the hips into the direction of attack in the previous actions.

Action 4: Visualize your opponent

blocking the attack in Action 3 and immediately counter with driving a second low-line strike with the first quarter of the staff.

Your target should be the opponent's rear leg or hand within the Angle 6 target area. Figures 47 and 48 illustrate this. Depending on the position of the opponent's leg, you may need to slide in and around to your left to acquire a good shot at that back leg. Practice this action along with Action 3 as one simultaneous one-two action, with one strike immediately following the other. Practice this in sets of 10–15 repetitions at slow speed before proceeding to medium and full speed.

Action 5: In this action you will attack the opponent's groin within the Angle 7 target area. First slide into the opponent, swinging the staff upward between his legs and drive forcefully upward as you pivot the hips to your right. You will be impacting on the fourth and third quarters of the staff, depending on how close the opponent is to you. Visualize yourself executing enough force to lift your opponent momentarily off the ground. To accomplish this, you will need to keep the right elbow tucked close to the body. Figure 49 illustrates this action.

Immediately after impact, swing the heel of the staff over and down into the Angle 8 target area, impacting on his head with the first quarter of the staff. As with the previous actions, perform both strikes as a one-two combination, going from low line immediately to high line. Figure 50 illustrates this action.

Action 6: After you have mastered the one-two combinations in Actions 1–5, you should practice them as one continuous exercise that begins with Action 1 and ends with Action 5. Practice these first from a static position, focusing on the hand and hip actions, and then repeat them while moving around the training area. Experiment with a variety of the footwork options discussed earlier, as well as shifting the hands along the length of the staff. This will give you a feel for the shifts necessary when moving from medium to close range. Rather than doing this action in sets, you may want to set a time limit and repeat the entire action with a one- to two-minute period. This will give you one fine cardio workout as, well as a feel for how position dictates the effectiveness of any given strike.

CHAPTER 6

ASPECTS OF STAFF TARGETING

Let's take a moment to look closer at the types of targets and associated results you can expect to achieve when you strike or thrust one of the targets within the target angle areas discussed previously. During his early research for the milestone publication *Contemporary Knife Targeting* (Paladin Press, 2006), Christopher Grosz gathered insights on edged-weapons targets and tactics from Michael Janich (with whom Grosz later teamed up to coauthor the book) and Datu Kelly Worden. Based on these insights, Grosz grouped the targets into six categories based on current medical knowledge: distraction, vascular, nervous system, structural, organ, and muscles. Although *Contemporary Knife Targeting* focuses on the effects of edged weapons, some of the information applies to the use of the staff. Before delving into these, let's reflect on the function of a staff—simply put, to knock the hell out of your opponent. Unless you enhance the staff with spear point and spikes, the staff relies on force and power to achieve this result.

DISTRACTION TARGETS

These are targets that, when hit, will disrupt the motion or concentration of the opponent. They may or may not be disabling and are used to provide an opportunity for an immediate follow-on attack. Due to its limited power, a short strike is particularly effective when used against the hands and head. Thrusts to the throat, abdomen, and groin can also create quite a distraction from the opponent's original intent. Figure 57 illustrates some common distraction targets for the staff.

VASCULAR TARGETS

Generally speaking, the staff does not work well against vascular targets because they are usually inside the body and in some cases are protected by bone or muscle. They are associated with the human circulatory system and composed of arteries and veins, the "plumbing" of the human body. Because the staff is an impact weapon, striking and thrusting that produce internal bleeding will not produce an immediate reaction, such as unconsciousness.

NERVOUS SYSTEM TARGETS

The spinal cord, brain stem, and brain fall into this category. The effect of a powerful strike or thrust will usually produce immediate results that can stun, render unconscious, or even kill an opponent. You might call these high-level nervous system

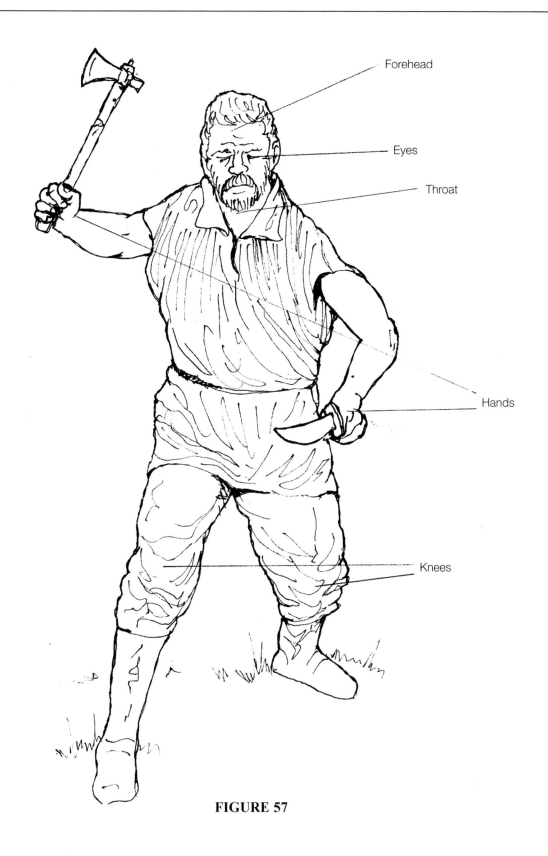

Forehead

Eyes

Throat

Hands

Knees

FIGURE 57

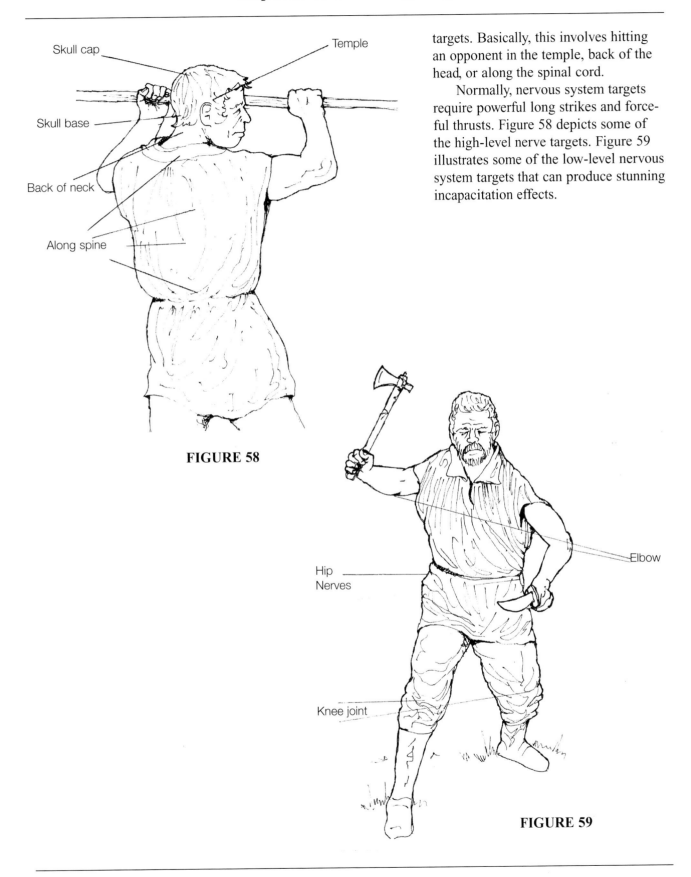

targets. Basically, this involves hitting an opponent in the temple, back of the head, or along the spinal cord.

Normally, nervous system targets require powerful long strikes and forceful thrusts. Figure 58 depicts some of the high-level nerve targets. Figure 59 illustrates some of the low-level nervous system targets that can produce stunning incapacitation effects.

FIGURE 58

FIGURE 59

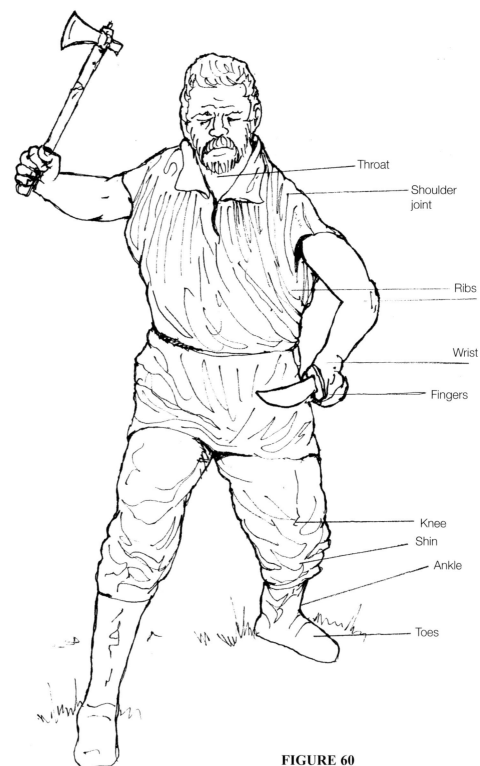

Throat

Shoulder
joint

Ribs

Wrist

Fingers

Knee

Shin

Ankle

Toes

**STRUCTURAL
TARGETS**

The skeletal structure
of the human body offers
prime targets for both long
and short strikes. These
break, crush, or fracture,
and generally damage the
surrounding muscle and
connective tissue. Joints
are primary targets that
will shut down an oppo-
nent's movement and tim-
ing. Figure 60 depicts
some of the common struc-
tural targets for the staff.

FIGURE 60

ORGAN TARGETS

Since most of these targets are contained inside the body, they are not immediately vulnerable to attack by impact weapons. Yes, damage to structural, nerve, and muscle targets create bleeding and swelling, and will indirectly affect them, but no real immediate results will occur. The eyes and testicles are the only exposed organs that will get an immediate reaction if hit. Figure 61 depicts these two targets. (As for female opponents, I have it on reliable information that it still hurts to get hit in the genitals.)

MUSCLE TARGETS

Delivering the proper amount of force through a strike or thrust to a muscle group can be almost as debilitating as severing it. Strikes to biceps, triceps, quadriceps, and associated tendons can greatly reduce an opponent's timing and movement. The primary muscle targets are included in Figure 62.

FIGURE 61

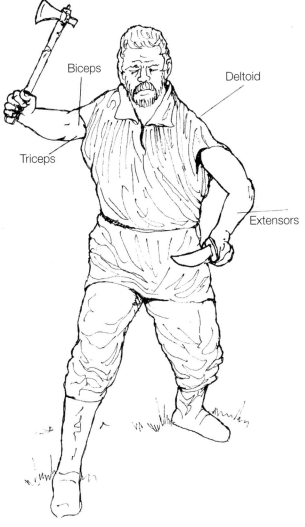

FIGURE 62

BOTTOM LINE FOR STAFF TARGETING

So where does all this targeting information leave us? First of all, it's pretty clear that the staff is an impact weapon, and some of the effects of a blow may not always be as immediate as those produced by an edged weapon. Yes, the staff can cause damage to all six target groups, but the most immediate result will be by attacking the structural and nervous system targets. The joints of the arms and legs become particularly important in disabling an opponent and setting the stage for a follow-on kill shot to the temple or base of the skull. A thrust to the eye and throat can also greatly reduce an opponent's will to fight. I don't say that this is a definite rule of thumb for staff targeting, but it definitely should be high on your consideration list.

Swinging-in-the-Breeze Striking

Now, let's get back to our striking exercises using the long-strike technique. In Training Objective 4 in the last chapter, you were executing the long strike into the air. While this "swinging-in-the-breeze" approach was good to give the initial feel for the way the weapon behaves, you can never develop any power for your strikes without actually hitting a target. In Training Objective 5 (page 63), you will explore hitting a target at slow, medium, and full speed.

TARGETING AND TRAINING TARGETS

Historically, the term *pell* has been used to identify stationary training targets for both soldiers and civilians in both edged- and impact-weapon training. Since ancient times, training targets have taken on a variety of forms, ranging from tree trunks and logs in the ground to the punching bags and synthetic human torso targets of today. I think the Roman military writer Flavius Vegetius Renatus (who

lived around 395 C.E.) gives us a good picture of how training targets are used:

> "[A] stake was planted in the ground by each recruit in such a manner that it projected six feet in height and could not sway. Against the stake the recruit practiced his wickerwork shield and wooden stick just as if he were fighting a real enemy. Sometimes he aimed against the head or the face, sometimes he threatened the flanks, sometimes he endeavored to strike down the knees and legs. He gave ground, he attacked, he assaulted, and he assailed the stake with all the skill and energy required in actual fighting."

A Standard Target (Pell)

This pretty much sums up where the next step in your staff training needs to go. To begin with, you're going to need some form of target you can beat on. Some of the early medieval manuscripts showed knights banging away at a tree trunk that had been stripped of leaves, so that's an option. Down in the woods by where I live there is a really large tree that a hurricane took the top out of several years back. About 20 feet tall and 48 inches in circumference,

Log or tree trunk

Rope or strapping tape

3 to 4 layers of worn carpet

FIGURE 63

the tree is completely dead and dry, with most of the bark gone. I throw tomahawks at it and use it as a pell for live steel work with the knife and sword.

I also have a smaller tree target that is 8 feet tall and 12 inches in circumference. I use this one more frequently because it allows me to move freely around it in the manner that Flavius describes. It is probably ideal for that purpose. I don't use the staff on it because of the damage that repeated strikes would cause to the weapon. If you want to use a target of this design, I recommend you pad it by wrapping it in several layers of old carpet taped together with duct or strapping tape. Figure 63 illustrates this.

I've also seen similar targets covered with sections of old tires, which work quite well if you don't mind your staff getting discolored from the rubber. Today there are a number of anatomically correct human silhouette targets on the market. These are a bit pricey but are very sturdy and allow you to direct your blows against realistic targets; they also do not damage your staff. I have had good results with these targets holding up to repeated use with wood, plastic, and aluminum training. Figure 64 depicts one such generic target.

FIGURE 64

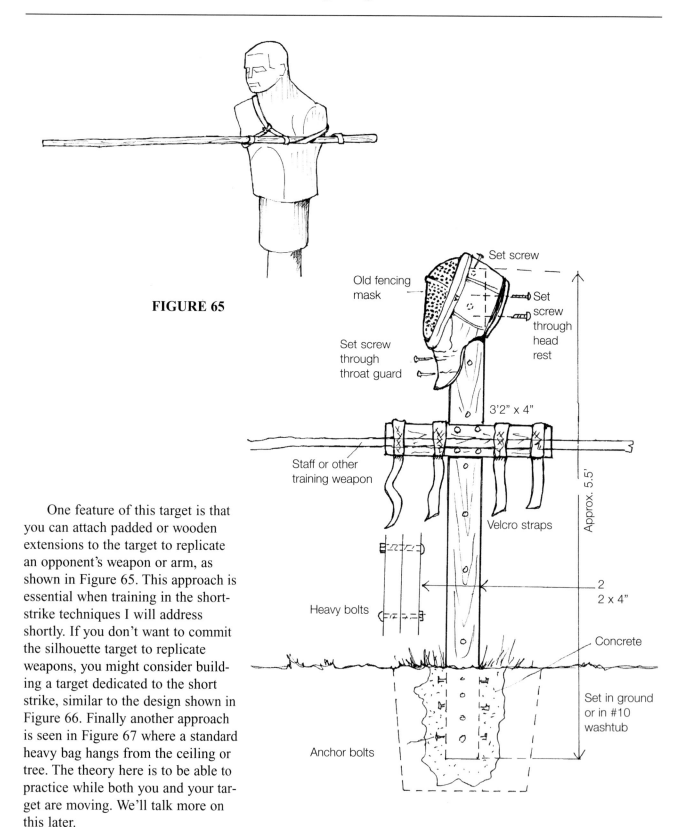

FIGURE 65

One feature of this target is that you can attach padded or wooden extensions to the target to replicate an opponent's weapon or arm, as shown in Figure 65. This approach is essential when training in the short-strike techniques I will address shortly. If you don't want to commit the silhouette target to replicate weapons, you might consider building a target dedicated to the short strike, similar to the design shown in Figure 66. Finally another approach is seen in Figure 67 where a standard heavy bag hangs from the ceiling or tree. The theory here is to be able to practice while both you and your target are moving. We'll talk more on this later.

FIGURE 66

FIGURE 67

TRAINING OBJECTIVE 5

Task: Execute the staff long strikes into the eight target areas on an anatomically correct human silhouette target.

Condition: You need a staff and training area sufficient to accommodate 360-degree movement and overhead strikes with the staff. Remember the exercise in Training Objective 3? You are going to repeat this same sequence, only this time your focus will be on the transition to the delivery of hard, forceful strikes to the various target areas.

Action 1: Begin by taking a middle-guard position approximately 10–15 feet away from the target. This should place you just out of range of an opponent armed with a similar staff. Begin the exercise by moving into position using either the forward or advancing steps discussed earlier. As you come into range, take a slight half step to your right and deliver a long strike into one of the targets in the Angle 1 area, as depicted in Figure 40. Immediately on impact, execute a long strike at one of the targets in the Angle 2 attack area. Execute both these strikes as a one-two attack, as discussed earlier. Visualize your opponent blocking your first strike, as illustrated in Figures 68 and 69, which will require you to immediately counter by delivering the strike into the Angle 2 area.

FIGURE 68

Focus on the push-pull and slight wringing action for the strike into the Angle 1 attack area. As you become more experienced with this technique, you will note that while you can accomplish this action all along the opponent's left side, it is difficult to do along his right side. On the right side, strikes tend to rely more on pulling action than wringing. You'll also find that strikes into Angle 2, 4, and 6 areas require more shoulder and hip action into the direction of attack.

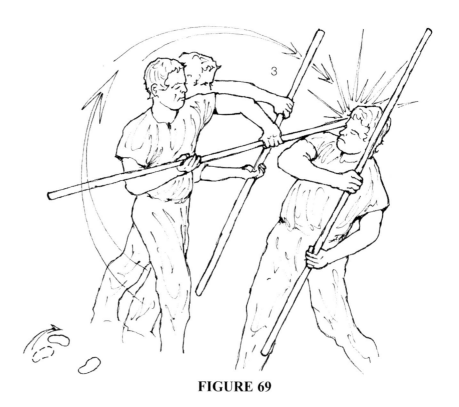

FIGURE 69

NOTE: Let's address movement for a moment. You will note that you began this exercise by moving into position to execute a strike. You can use any of the footwork patterns addressed earlier. Once you are in range to attack, the footwork diagrams on Figures 40–53 (pages 40–44) are there to demonstrate the positioning of the feet during delivery of the strike. Keep in mind that it may be necessary to take an additional step forward or back to achieve the optimum position. Now, don't get so focused on footwork that you lose sight of what you are really doing: using distance, time, and position to deliver an attack. Never think of it as "my feet must be here or there." Rather, look at it as "I must move to this position." You already know how to walk and run, and since childhood you have been practicing this bipedal balancing act that humans do. Center your body over your feet and think of "position," and your feet will do their job. Remember too that you can attack with the staff moving both forward and to the rear.

Action 2: On completion of Action 1, execute a passing step backward to the right, and visualize your opponent closing rapidly on you. Move your right hand into the third quarter and the left into the fourth quarter of the staff.

While twisting your hips violently, execute a close-range strike into the Angle 3 area, targeting your opponent's hips or elbow. Remember to pull the staff tight against the body in the vicinity of the hips. Don't forget to slightly flex the legs on initiation, when you will be driving upward on impact. As with Action 1, immediately execute the same strike from the left into the Angle 4 area. On completion of this strike, bring your staff back to center and push into your opponent's weapon as you step backward out of the window of combat.

Action 3: As you complete Action 2 with that backward step, shift your hands back to their middle-guard position on the staff and execute an ascending strike into the Angle 5 area. Immediately swing the right leg to the rear, twist the hips, and execute another ascending strike into the Angle 6 area.

Action 4: Visualize your opponent taking a step backward as he raises his staff. Taking advantage of this opening, you slide in close and deliver an ascending strike upward into the groin area in the Angle 7 area. Remember, this strike is almost vertical, so if possible attempt to lift the opponent off the ground with a violent push-pull action. (On most targets you will find the supporting pole of the base is in the way of this strike, so you should strike to the left or right of this obstruction.) Immediately visualize your opponent's violent downward block halting your attack. You immediately push the heel of the staff over and down, executing a descending strike with the left hand into the Angle 8 area. This completes the targeting drill.

Standard: You should practice this entire exercise first at slow speed with light impact until you become comfortable and accurate. As your proficiency improves, gradually increase the speed and force of your attacks. As with Training Objective 3, you should vary the targets within each angle area each time you initiate a new repetition. For example, on one set you might attack the opponent's temple in Angle 1 and his elbow in Angle 2; on the next set try hitting the collarbone and right temple, respectively. You should strive to complete all the actions of this exercise at least 10 times daily until you become proficient.

TRAINING OBJECTIVE 6

Task: Execute the staff short strikes into eight target areas.

Condition: You need a staff and training area sufficient to accommodate 360-degree movement and overhead strikes with the weapon. The point of this exercise is to become familiar with using the short strike to disrupt attacks and gain openings for the more devastating long strikes. Like Training Objective 3, these strikes will be into the open air; consequently the use of a wall chart depicting a full-size human silhouette (Figure 39, page 39) will be beneficial as a directional guide for your attacks. You can accomplish this also in front of a mirror on your own reflection. Don't be concerned initially with delivering hard, fast strikes; rather, just complete each action slowly and smoothly, focusing on the correct swing and footwork.

Standard:

Action 1: Start off in a middle-guard position. Now, do a quick scan of Figures 70–78. You will find two types of illustrations that show the approximate position of the short-strike delivery from the side and from a position directly in front of your opponent. In all examples, you will be using the "floating staff" drawing to give an idea of where the strike will be going. Keep in mind that these drawings are conceptual and just can't represent the speed of the short strike. For learning purposes, I have exaggerated the slight lift that occurs just prior to the strike.

Remember, it is a low, flat trajectory, not unlike that of a thrust followed by a violent push-pull action of the hand that snaps the tip into the target area. Visualize your opponent in front of you armed with a staff, as depicted in Figure 70. As you close to him, note that he does not take any evasive action; he merely shifts his body to his left to continue facing you. Once you are within range, execute a short strike to his lead right hand. On impact, immediately lift your tip slightly, swinging across to your right, and make a second short strike to his rear left hand as

you continue your forward movement. The rhythm for these strikes might sound like "Bam! Bam!"

This is a very quick and effective method for damaging your opponent's hands and maybe even forcing him to drop his weapon (Figures 71 and 72). As soon as you complete the second short strike, immediately bring your tip back to the center just in case he attempts to counterattack.

FIGURE 70

FIGURE 71

FIGURE 72

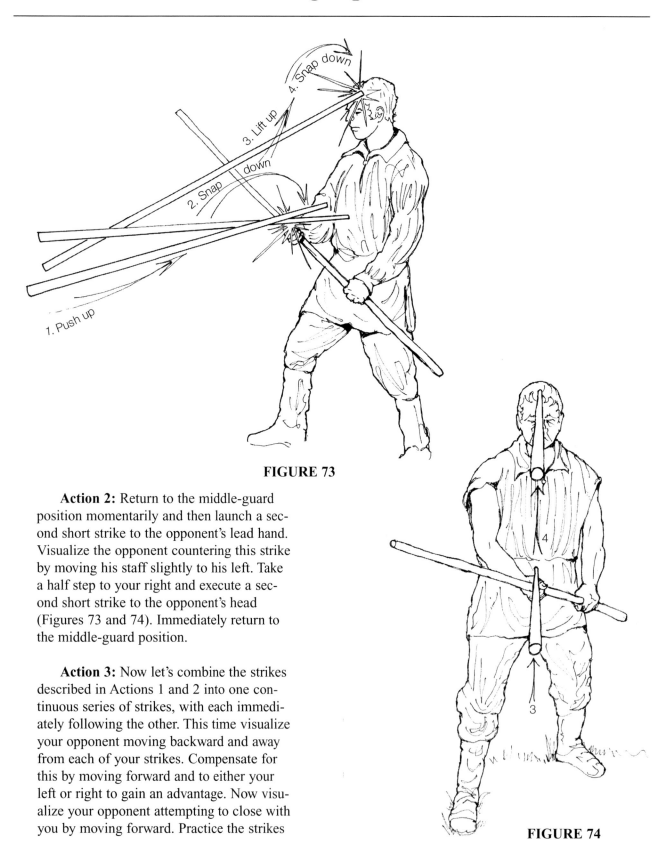

FIGURE 73

Action 2: Return to the middle-guard position momentarily and then launch a second short strike to the opponent's lead hand. Visualize the opponent countering this strike by moving his staff slightly to his left. Take a half step to your right and execute a second short strike to the opponent's head (Figures 73 and 74). Immediately return to the middle-guard position.

Action 3: Now let's combine the strikes described in Actions 1 and 2 into one continuous series of strikes, with each immediately following the other. This time visualize your opponent moving backward and away from each of your strikes. Compensate for this by moving forward and to either your left or right to gain an advantage. Now visualize your opponent attempting to close with you by moving forward. Practice the strikes

FIGURE 74

in Action 1 while stepping backward first to your left and then right. Immediately move forward and execute an Action 2 while moving forward. Don't worry about doing this exactly as I described; feel free to change this sequence by varying the strikes and positions you assume.

Action 4: In this action you visualize an opponent armed with two weapons similar to those depicted in Figure 76: a long knife in his left hand and a tomahawk in his right. It's pretty clear that an opponent thus equipped will probably thrust with the long knife and strike with the tomahawk. You'll note that he holds his tomahawk high above his head in sort of a high-guard position. Let there be no doubt in your mind that the tomahawk is going to come down like a bat out of hell toward your head. Yes, that long

knife point can come almost as fast during a thrust, but notice that he is holding the knife in his left hand and his left leg is in the rear position. You'll have to be close to him to provoke that thrust, and it will be necessary for him to adjust his position slightly just prior to launching. That action will probably telegraph his intention. That tomahawk is the obvious threat and likely to do the most damage if it connects.

Suddenly, your opponent slides forward and begins the strike with the tomahawk. Slide back slightly and execute a short strike to his incoming hand. Immediately on impact, withdraw your tip, swing it across to your right, and execute a second short strike to his left knife-bearing hand (Figures 75 and 76).

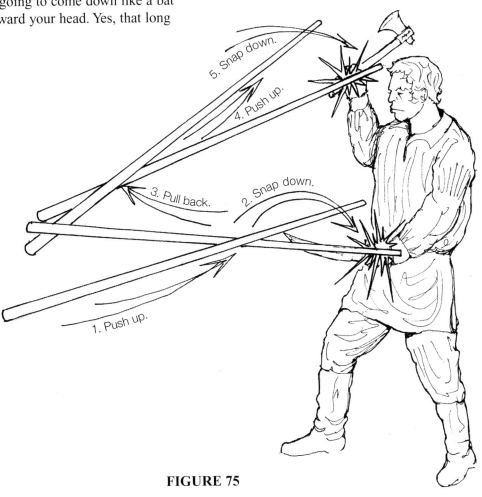

FIGURE 75

FIGURE 76

FIGURE 77

FIGURE 78

Action 5: Let's try another approach against this same scenario. Visualize your opponent attacking with a thrust from the long knife first. As in Action 4, slide back, but this time to your right, and deliver a short strike to the side of the opponent's incoming hand. Immediately lift your tip up and to your left and deliver a second short strike to your opponent's head (Figures 77 and 78).

NOTE: Practice each of the actions separately until you become familiar with the rhythm and mechanics of delivering each of the sequences. Don't be in a hurry—remember, you are just striking into the air to get a feel for the dynamics of the short strike. As mentioned earlier, you can use a wall chart or mirror to get used to striking the respective target areas. You need to devote about 15 minutes to this training regimen. When you are proficient, move on to executing all five actions, one after the other with no break in between. Begin to work this from slow to full speed until that short snap becomes second nature. Remember, this is one of the primary disruption techniques for the staff at medium range. When you get comfortable with this aspect, you should begin to think about following each of the short strikes with a more powerful long strike that will take your opponent out of the fight.

TRAINING OBJECTIVE 7

Task: Execute staff short-strikes at full force into target areas.

Condition: You need a staff and training area sufficient to accommodate 360-degree movement and overhead strikes with the weapon. Figure 79 depicts two hand targets that your training partner can use to accurately replicate the scenarios discussed in Training Objective 5. These are made with a core of quarter-inch PVC pipe covered with two layers of pipe insulation and secured with a layer of duct or strapping tape. They simulate your opponent's hand and head position, and provide the opportunity to move the targets toward the student in reasonable safety. Although these illustrations do not show head protection, it is a good idea to wear such in case someone misses the target. The point of this exercise is to become familiar with actually hitting a target using full-force short strikes to disrupt attacks and gain openings for the more devastating long strikes.

Standard:

Action 1: Take a position in front of your training partner just within striking range. Your training partner should assume the position depicted in Figure 79, with his arms slightly chambered. He begins the action by extending his right arm, pushing the hand target forward about a foot toward the student. This simulates an opponent shifting his weapon to gain an advantage. On sensing his movement, you should deliver a short strike to the lead target and then shift the tip to the right and deliver a second strike to the left-hand target. Immediately, retract the staff and move to your opponent's left or right. Figures 80 and 81 depict this action.

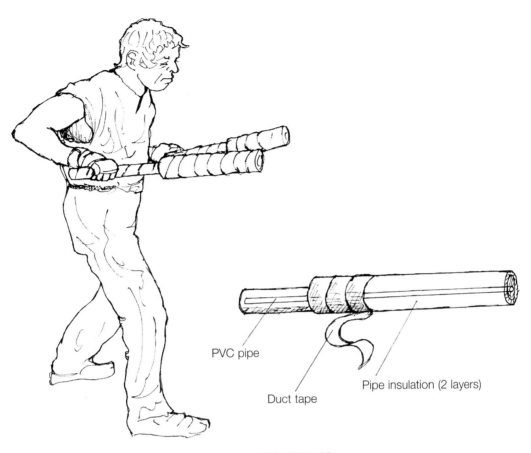

PVC pipe

Duct tape

Pipe insulation (2 layers)

FIGURE 79

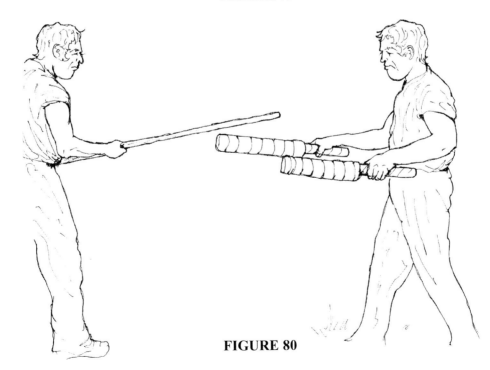

FIGURE 80

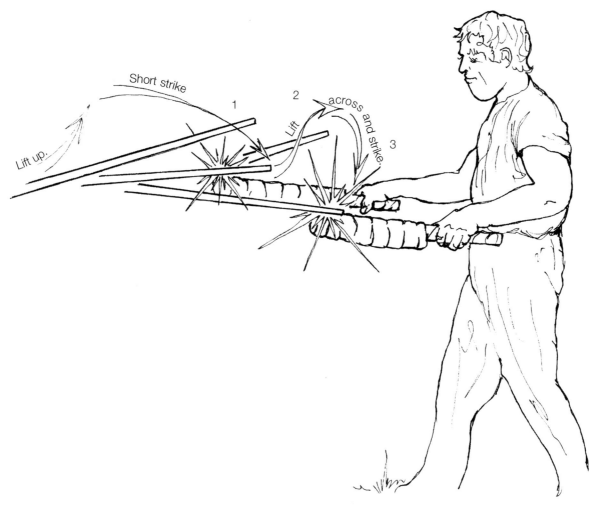

FIGURE 81

Action 2: Your training partner adjusts his position to your move and then raises the left-hand target up in line with his head while leaving the right hand target in its original position. As soon as your partner raises the left-hand target, deliver a short strike first to the training partner's right-hand target. Immediately follow with a short strike to the raised left-hand target (which simulates the opponent's head). Figure 82 depicts this action. Move back into the middle-guard position.

Action 3: Your training partner moves his right-hand target up in line with his head and extends his left-hand target slightly forward. On sensing this movement, immediately deliver a short strike to the partner's left-hand target and immediately follow with one to the raised right-hand target. On completion of this strike, immediately move back to the middle guard. Figure 83 depicts this action.

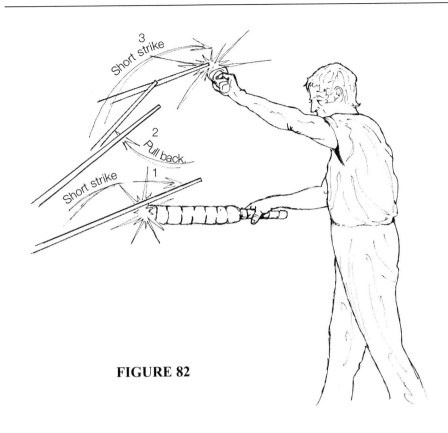

FIGURE 82

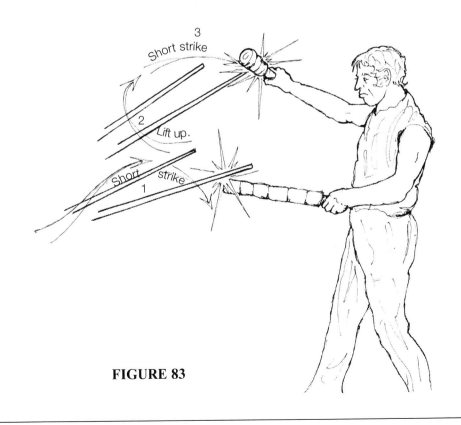

FIGURE 83

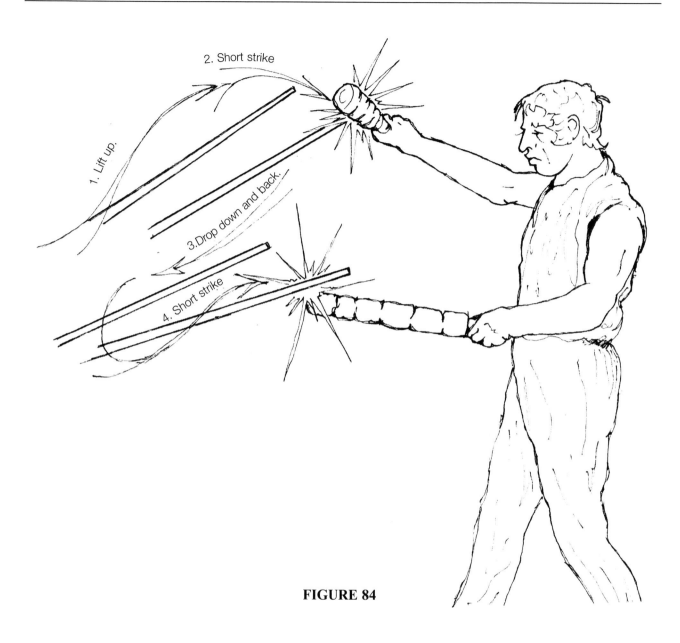

2. Short strike

1. Lift up.

3. Drop down and back.

4. Short strike

FIGURE 84

Action 4: While your training partner maintains the same position in Action 3, deliver a short strike to the raised right-hand target and follow by dropping your tip and delivering a second strike to the left-hand target (Figure 84).

NOTE: Repeat all four actions in sets of 10 to 15 until you become proficient. As with the other exercises, begin by using only moderate force and then as you acquire skill move on to full force.

CHAPTER 7
ASPECTS OF LONG-GRIP STRIKES

Let's examine for a moment strikes as delivered from the long grip. I'm doing this not to say that the long grip is inferior to that of the other hand positions, but rather to make you aware of the advantages of this grip in the context of being able to work all parts of the staff.

Note that the left hand is positioned on the heel of the staff in the first quarter and the right is in the middle of the second quarter. Figure 85 depicts common guards for the long grip with the right leg forward. Remember, the hands reverse themselves when the left leg is leading. The long grip places most of the staff in front of you and consequently requires a different manipulation than used earlier with the other grips.

Although short strikes with the long grip are identical to the other grips discussed, long strikes are delivered in a manner not unlike those used with a sword. The bottom line is that with a staff 6–8 feet in length, you've got a lot of wood to handle. The concept of

the one-two combination is limited to the fist of the rear hand, with most of the strike being delivered with the third and fourth quarters of the weapon.

I think it's pretty obvious that the long grip is for long range. Figure 86 depicts some of the striking limitations associated with the long grip. Take a

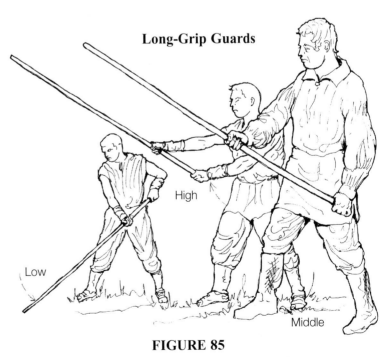

Long-Grip Guards

High

Low

Middle

FIGURE 85

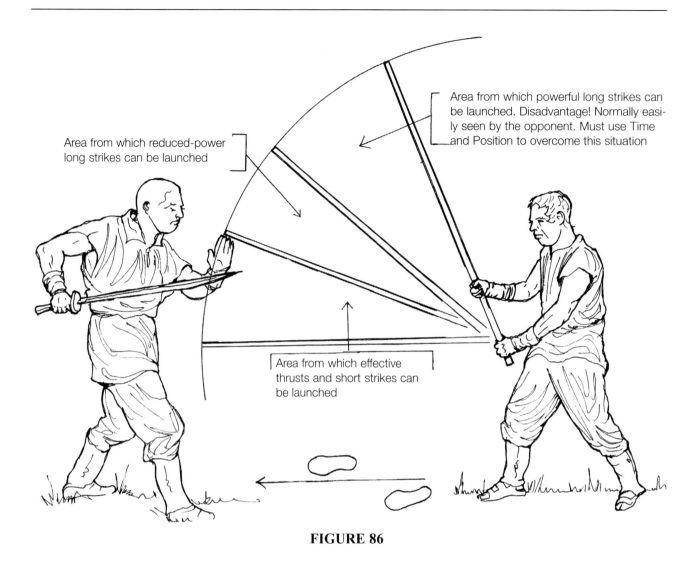

Area from which reduced-power long strikes can be launched

Area from which powerful long strikes can be launched. Disadvantage! Normally easily seen by the opponent. Must use Time and Position to overcome this situation

Area from which effective thrusts and short strikes can be launched

FIGURE 86

look at the descending arc in the illustration. Note that to really achieve powerful strikes, the staff must be moved up into that higher part of the arc. Yes, you can deliver solid strikes from the lower positions on the arc but nothing like those achieved from the higher positions. Basically, you have to always consider getting the tip of the staff into this area to deliver a strike. This results in somewhat of a "cocking action," which can easily be seen by the opponent. To avoid this cue, use timing and movement to get into position for delivery without telegraphing your action to your opponent.

Figure 87 shows an example of this, where the

man with the staff waits until his sword-wielding opponent attacks. As the opponent's blow comes in, he pivots off line to his left while simultaneously raising his staff into position. As the sword goes by, the staff man delivers a powerful Angle 8 strike to the opponent's head or arm.

Another method for moving the staff is depicted in Figure 88. This illustrates how the staff can be rolled backward and over into the Angle 1 attack area. (**NOTE:** The position of the staff in Action 2 of the illustration can also be used to deflect/block an opponent's incoming attack.)

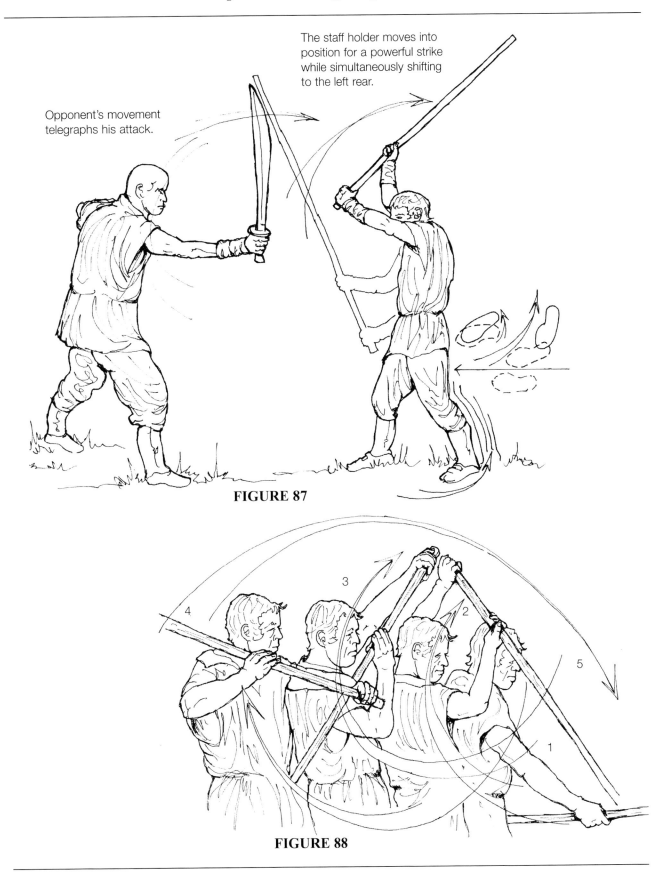

Opponent's movement telegraphs his attack.

The staff holder moves into position for a powerful strike while simultaneously shifting to the left rear.

FIGURE 87

FIGURE 88

FIGURE 89

In Figure 89 the same rolling action can be used by moving the rear hand across the torso to your right and pushing a forceful strike into Angle 2 target area. Remember that both of the methods used in Figures 88 and 89 are enhanced by movement outside the box.

Remember that with the hands on the first part of the 1st and 2nd quarters of the staff, you were able to deliver the one-two combination strikes into target areas on the left and right side of the opponent. The training approach for the long grip will be slightly different. This following exercise will execute long strikes down the opponent's left side, effect a hand change, and repeat the process down his right. Remember this is simply an exercise designed to familiarize you with the long grip strikes into all eight target areas.

TRAINING OBJECTIVE 8

Task: Execute the staff long strikes with a long grip into the eight target areas.

Condition: You need a staff and training area sufficient to accommodate 360-degree movement and overhead strikes with the weapon. You might consider practicing this exercise in front of a mirror or wall chart, as described in previous exercises. The point of this exercise is to become familiar with the delivery of long strikes with a long grip. Do not be concerned initially with hard, fast delivery. Rather, execute the strikes at slow speed before gradually progressing to full speed. This exercise is not intended to advocate the total use of the long grip, but rather to demonstrate the advantages of using the entire length of the staff as opportunity presents itself.

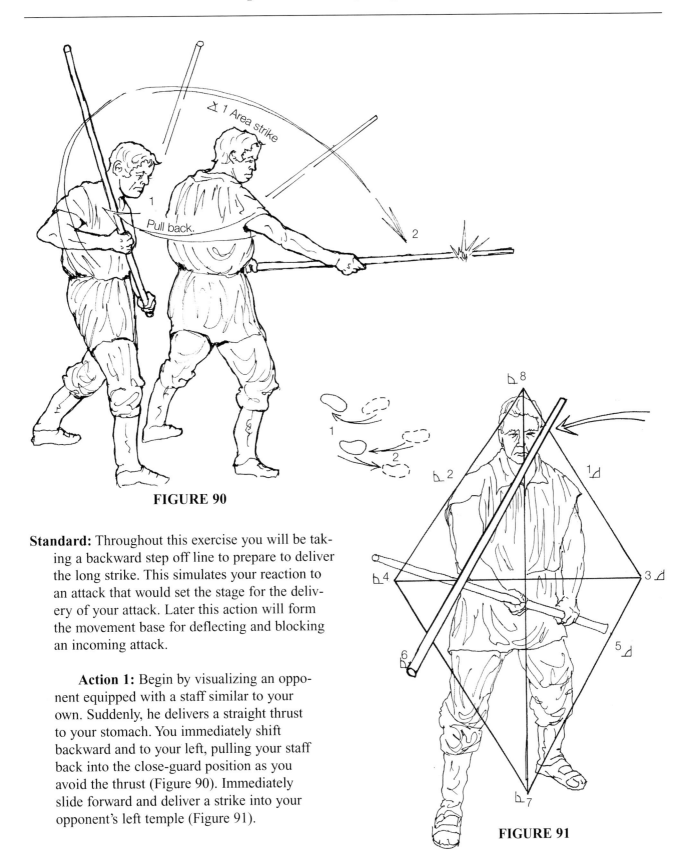

FIGURE 90

FIGURE 91

Standard: Throughout this exercise you will be taking a backward step off line to prepare to deliver the long strike. This simulates your reaction to an attack that would set the stage for the delivery of your attack. Later this action will form the movement base for deflecting and blocking an incoming attack.

   Action 1: Begin by visualizing an opponent equipped with a staff similar to your own. Suddenly, he delivers a straight thrust to your stomach. You immediately shift backward and to your left, pulling your staff back into the close-guard position as you avoid the thrust (Figure 90). Immediately slide forward and deliver a strike into your opponent's left temple (Figure 91).

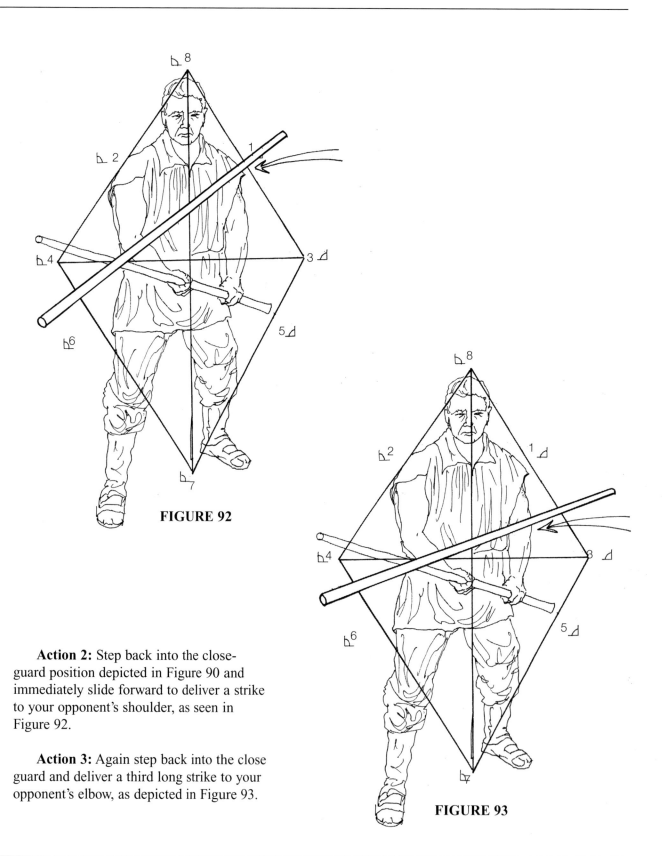

FIGURE 92

FIGURE 93

Action 2: Step back into the close-guard position depicted in Figure 90 and immediately slide forward to deliver a strike to your opponent's shoulder, as seen in Figure 92.

Action 3: Again step back into the close guard and deliver a third long strike to your opponent's elbow, as depicted in Figure 93.

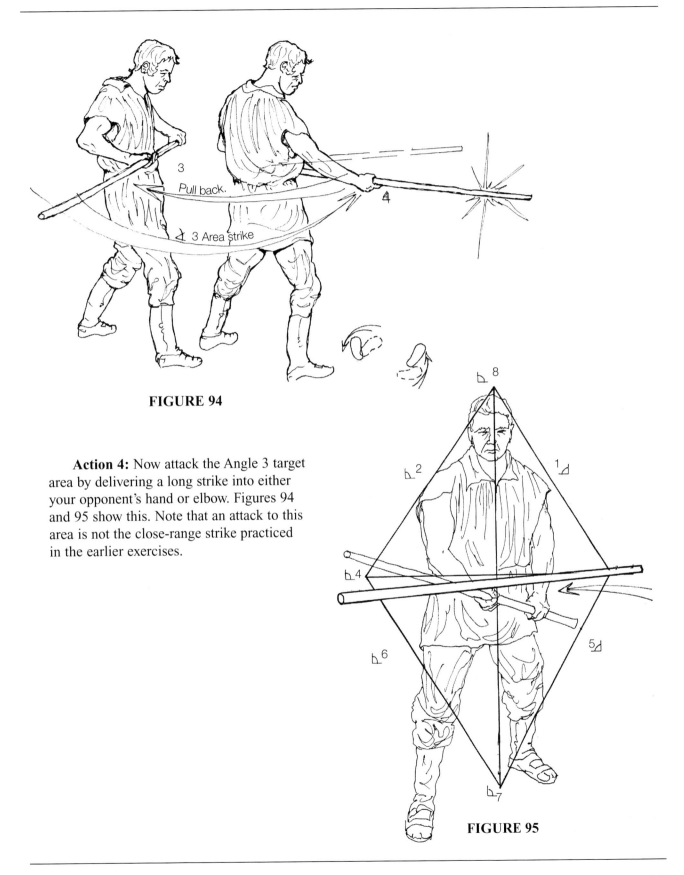

FIGURE 94

Action 4: Now attack the Angle 3 target area by delivering a long strike into either your opponent's hand or elbow. Figures 94 and 95 show this. Note that an attack to this area is not the close-range strike practiced in the earlier exercises.

FIGURE 95

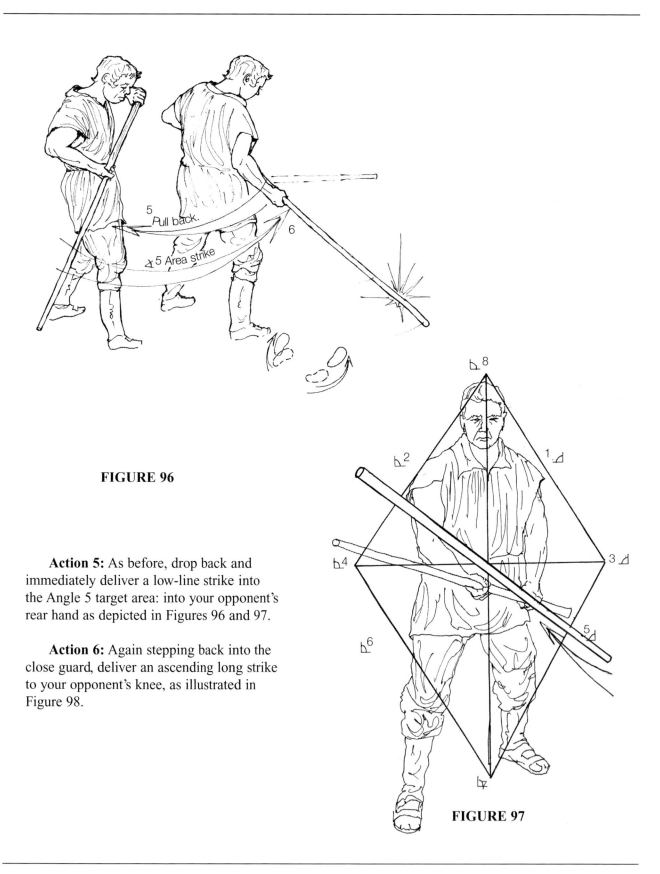

FIGURE 96

Action 5: As before, drop back and immediately deliver a low-line strike into the Angle 5 target area: into your opponent's rear hand as depicted in Figures 96 and 97.

Action 6: Again stepping back into the close guard, deliver an ascending long strike to your opponent's knee, as illustrated in Figure 98.

FIGURE 97

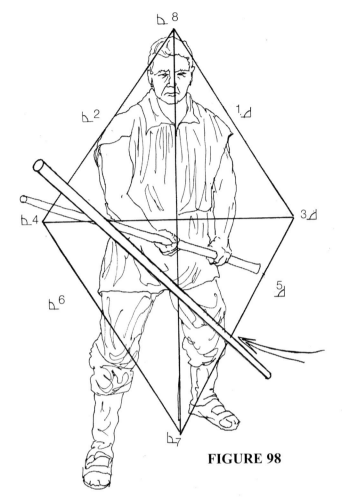

FIGURE 98

Action 7: This time instead of withdrawing, step forward and execute a hand change that puts your left leg forward. From this position, repeat the same strike sequence for Angles 2–6 target areas using the same rhythm of withdrawing, moving off line, and striking.

NOTE: Repeat this exercise 10–15 times until you are proficient.

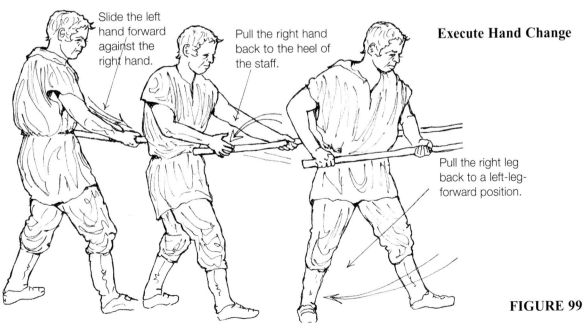

Slide the left hand forward against the right hand.

Pull the right hand back to the heel of the staff.

Execute Hand Change

Pull the right leg back to a left-leg-forward position.

FIGURE 99

TRAINING OBJECTIVE 9

Task: Execute the staff long strikes with a long grip into the eight target areas.

Condition: You need a staff and training area sufficient to accommodate 360-degree movement and overhead strikes with the weapon. You might consider practicing this exercise in front of a mirror or wall chart as in previous exercises. The point of this exercise is to become familiar with the delivery of long strikes with a long grip. Do not be concerned with hard fast, delivery initially. Rather, execute the strikes at slow speed before gradually progressing to full speed. This exercise is not intended to advocate the exclusive use of the long grip, but rather to demonstrate the advantages of using the entire length of the staff as opportunity presents itself.

Standard: Go back and review the technique demonstrated in Figure 88. Throughout this exercise you will be using this rolling technique to deliver the long strike using the long grip. As with Training Objective 8, this simulates reaction to an opponent's action in order to set the stage for delivery of your attack. Later this action will form the movement base for deflecting and blocking incoming attacks.

Actions 1–6: Repeat the same attacks addressed in Training Objective 8, using the technique demonstrated in Figure 88. But instead of stepping back, step to the left to get off line and deliver each respective strike.

Action 7: As before, on the completion of Action 5, execute a hand change that puts the left leg forward and repeat the process down the target areas on the opponent's right side.

NOTE: Repeat this exercise 10–15 times until you are proficient.

TRAINING OBJECTIVE 10

Task: Execute the rolling technique to deliver a long strike with the long grip.

Condition: You need a staff and training area sufficient to accommodate 360-degree movement and overhead strikes with the weapon. You might consider practicing this exercise in front of a mirror or wall chart as you did in the previous exercises. Remember the technique in Figure 88 where the staff was moved through a guard position to deliver a rolling strike? It can be performed on both the left and right sides without the grip change discussed earlier. Refer to Figures 100 and 101 as you go through the actions.

Standard:

Action 1: Begin in a middle-guard position, visualizing an opponent delivering a straight thrust to your midsection. While simultaneously shifting your torso off line, push the heel of the staff up and to your right. Push against the opponent's incoming weapon to your right and roll the staff tip up and over into an Angle 1 target area (Figure 100).

Action 2: Recover from the first strike by pushing the staff up and to your left, simulating pushing your opponent's weapon aside. As with Action 1, continue to roll the tip of the staff up and over into a second strike while stepping forward (Figure 101).
NOTE: Repeat this exercise 10–15 times until you become proficient.

Action 3: Now that you are familiar with this rolling technique, let's use it while moving forward and backward. Take up a good middle guard and begin with the first strike, stepping forward on the second strike and continuing this action for approximately 15 feet. Then execute the same strikes while moving backward. Experiment with the different variations of the footwork patterns addressed earlier.

FIGURE 100

FIGURE 101

CHAPTER 8
ASPECTS OF THE BACK STRIKE

When you compare sword cuts to staff strikes, it becomes readily apparent that hand movements along the staff do not require the same technical manipulation skill that makes one "edge aware" in the use of the sword. This is probably seen best in the use of a technique call the "back strike." The cleanest explanation for a back strike with the staff is simply striking back along the same line of an earlier strike or movement. This usually involves a pulling action back into the target area. Frequently, this technique is used after deliberately missing the first blow by pulling the staff back toward the body. When the tip has cleared the target area, push the staff forward and then pull it violently back into the target area along the same line. Figure 102 illustrates the back strike into the high-line area while Figure 103 provides a more detailed look at the mechanics.

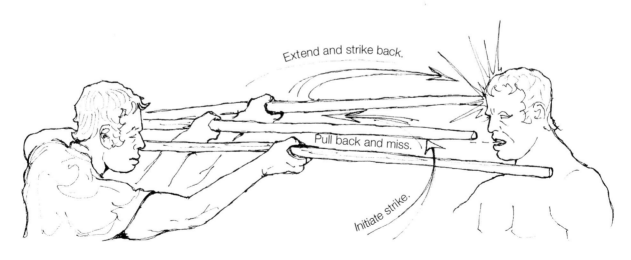

FIGURE 102

1. Strike and miss.

2. Pull back.

3. Push out.

4. Pull back.

FIGURE 103

Remember that this technique can be used in all target areas by the deliberate-miss method of simply positioning the staff to deliver the back strike. These approaches are particularly effective against joints or structure targets that become accessible when an opponent moves to a new position. Note that the back strike can be delivered using any of the grips and guards discussed earlier.

TRAINING OBJECTIVE 11

Task: Execute the back strike technique in conjunction with deliberately missing the target with an initial strike.

Condition: You need a staff and training area sufficient to accommodate 360-degree movement and overhead strikes with the weapon. Although you can practice the back strike in the air, to really develop a feel for the technique it is best to use a heavy bag or silhouette target. You may also use a padded pell.

Standard:

Action 1: Begin with a middle-guard position in front of the target. Initiate a strike into the Angle 1 target area. As the strike goes forward, pull the tip of the staff back to the point where it just clears the intended target area, somewhere near the left side of the opponent's neck. As the tip clears the target, extend the staff back onto line and violently pull the staff back along the same line into the right side of the opponent's neck.

Action 2: Immediately execute a strike into the Angle 2 target area with the heel of the staff (one-two concept). As the strike goes forward, pull the heel back to the point where it just clears the target area on the right side of the opponent's neck. As the heel clears the target, push the staff forward onto line and violently pull back, striking the left side of the opponent's neck.

Action 3: Repeat Actions 1 and 2 for target areas 1–6, visualizing the variety of potential structural targets that this technique can be used against. Also begin to think about how these techniques would work against an opponent equipped with other types of weapons.

Action 4: After you have your striking proficiency up to speed, begin to experiment with a variety of footwork movements that take you inside and outside the box of your opponent. Look for positions where a simple circular turn can provide an advantage for the back strike.

CHAPTER 9
ASPECTS OF THE REVERSE GRIP

Continuing with the theme of working all parts of the staff, we will now look at what, for lack of a better term, is called the reverse grip. Figure 104 depicts two typical reverse-grip stances. The Japanese refer to this as *gedan no kamae* (small illustration), a posture from which very effective low-line attacks can be made into the legs and groin area. You can perform it with either leg forward and with the weapon on either side of the body. The hands can be in a mixed or both-palms-down grip, with the lead hand on the heel of the staff with the tip trailing. If you have a staff that has a particularly heavy heel, you can reverse this, with that portion trailing to give additional heft to your strike. For illustrative purposes, use the large illustration in Figure 104 to depict the starting position of your strikes.

The most obvious feature of this reverse-grip technique is that you do not have much wood to the front facing your opponent. Strikes with this approach are ascending and may shift off line with a slight angle, depending on where the target areas are located. Figure 105 depicts a strike into the high-line area of the Angle 1 target area. The strike is performed with a push-and-pull action from the lead and trail hand, respectively, as depicted in Figure 106.

FIGURE 104

FIGURE 105

The strike may be executed at medium or close range by extending or pulling the arms close to the body during the initial execution of the strike. I see these strikes being executed as part of a transition from either a middle- or high-guard position in reaction to some action or target opening created by the opponent. For example, your opponent executes an overhead strike to your head. Immediately, you shift off line and move to the rear with a passing step backward. Simultaneously, you shift your hands to the reverse grip and deliver a powerful upward strike to your opponent's extended arms. I'll talk more about this during the section on engagement scenarios. For now, let's practice striking with the reverse grip to get a feel for the power associated with the technique.

TRAINING OBJECTIVE 12

Task: Execute the reverse grip strike technique

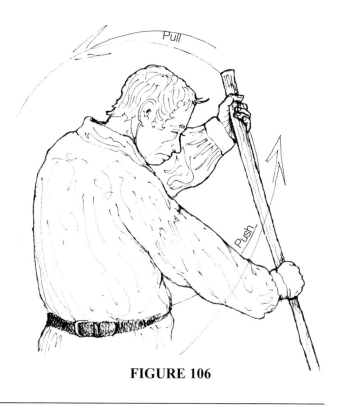

FIGURE 106

FIGURE 107

Condition: You need a staff and training area sufficient to accommodate 360-degree movement and overhead strikes with the weapon. You should practice the reverse grip technique first in the air and then move on to using a heavy bag or pell.

Standard:

Action 1: Begin with the reverse-grip position depicted in Figure 104. Execute a reverse-grip strike to the Angle 1 target area and then immediately pull back and off line, assuming the original starting position. This action is illustrated in Figure 107, while Figure 108 depicts the strike from your view.

FIGURE 108

FIGURE 109

Action 2: As soon as the start position is assumed, immediately deliver a second ascending strike into the Angle 3 target area, as depicted in Figures 109 and 110. As before, when you have completed the strike, move back off line to the original guard.

Action 3: Once in the original position, deliver a third strike into the Angle 5 target area and then move back to the original position. This action is illustrated in Figures 111 and 112.

FIGURE 110

FIGURE 111

Action 4: On completion of Action 3, execute a hand change, shifting the staff to the left side of your body and place the right hand as the lead hand. This change is accomplished exactly as what you did earlier from the middle-guard position, except that you have no length of staff in front of you. When this is done, repeat actions 1–3 for your opponent's right side, targeting areas 2, 4, and 6.

Action 5: Once you are familiar with the reverse-grip technique, repeat the same actions using a heavy bag or pell.

NOTE: This objective should be practiced from 10 to 15 times until you have become proficient.

FIGURE 112

CHAPTER 10
ASPECTS OF THE THRUST

Although the staff is generally thought of as an impact weapon, its potential for thrusting is remarkable. The late 17th-century fencing master Joseph Swetnam believed that with the addition of a spike, the staff was superior to most weapons of the time. Clearly, this thought was shared by many other Renaissance masters who saw the staff as a starting point for transition to many of the other polearms of the time.

The fact that most staff techniques can be used for the spear is evident in the application of the thrust. There are basically two methods of thrusting with the tip of the staff: the two-handed thrust and the single-handed thrust. Figure 113 illustrates the two-handed thrust, which can be delivered with either leg forward. Figure 113A depicts the thrust being delivered from the right side with the left leg forward; 113B illustrates the method from the left side with the right leg forward.

These thrusts begin with the middle guard and involve pushing the tip forward and upward at a slight ascending angle into one of the common target areas depicted in Figure 114. During the execution, it is best to think of these thrusts as a push or an extension of the weapon. There is no lunge associated with this technique, but rather the feet are

A

B

FIGURE 113

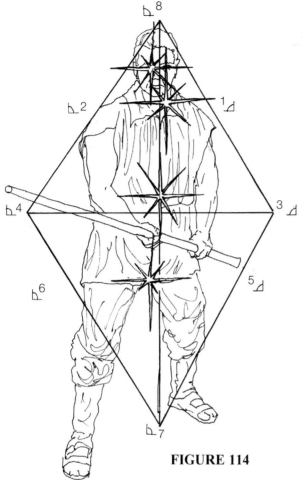

FIGURE 114

simply shifted forward or backward, which puts your weight behind the thrust. Figure 115 depicts the single-handed thrust as it is delivered from the left and right side with either leg forward.

While the foot work for this thrust is identical to the two-handed thrust, this technique can be delivered off a passing step with either leg forward. This technique is not unlike that used with Greek and Roman spears. The single-hand thrust normally begins in a middle guard and is delivered by pushing the tip forward into the target with the rear hand, while simultaneously releasing the lead hand. The key to effective delivery is finding the balance point on the staff, as seen in Figure 116.

Normally, with a middle guard only a slight adjustment of the hand is required; however, if the staff has a very heavy tip or heel, it may be necessary to shift the hand forward or backward in an action similar to that illustrated in Figure 117. The thrust can also be delivered using the heel of the staff. In military bayonet techniques, this is referred to as *a horizontal butt stroke* and is very effective when used in conjunction with two-handed and single-handed strikes as a follow-up technique. Figure 118 illustrates this thrust; Figures 119 and 120 illustrate its being used as follow-on for a single-handed thrust. The execution of this thrust begins by a

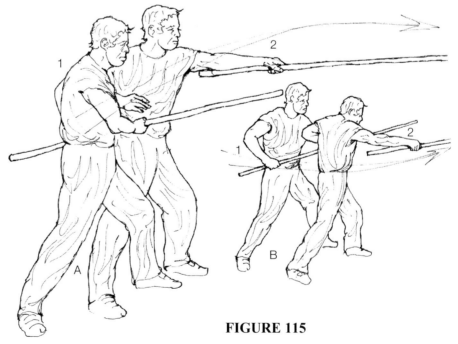

FIGURE 115

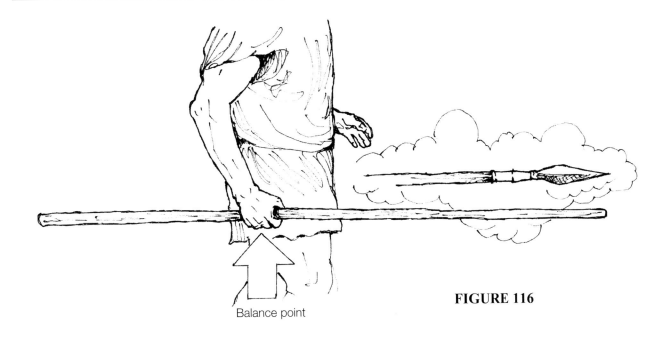

FIGURE 116

Balance point

Thrust

FIGURE 117

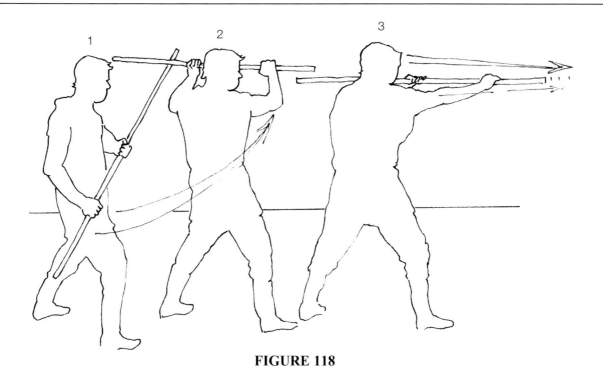

FIGURE 118

sweeping or striking action that crosses the chest and moves the arms upward into position with the heel facing the opponent. The heel is driven straight forward into the target area and then immediately retracted or chambered back for initiation of another attack. Here it is important to note that with all thrusts, the staff strikes out and is immediately pulled back and never left on the target area.

FIGURE 119

FIGURE 120

TRAINING OBJECTIVE 13

Task: Execute the two-handed thrust with the staff into three primary target areas.

Condition: You need a staff and training area sufficient to accommodate 360-degree movement and overhead strikes with the weapon. You may use a heavy bag, silhouette target, or padded pell.

Standard: The purpose of this drill is to improve proficiency in executing the two-handed thrust from middle-guard positions with either the right or left leg forward and the staff positioned accordingly. Take up a middle-guard position within striking distance of the target. Remember that this technique does not require you to cover a large distance by lunging forward as a fencer might. Rather, it is about getting within the proper range, where you simply slide forward and push the tip into the target. Throughout this training objective, think about the possibility of following each thrust with either a strike or movement outside the box.

Action 1: Slide forward and violently drive the thrust into the opponent's forehead. Immediately pull back to the middle guard and execute a second thrust to the throat of the opponent. Repeat chambering back into the middle guard a third time and execute a thrust to the opponent's groin. Figure 121 illustrates this process.

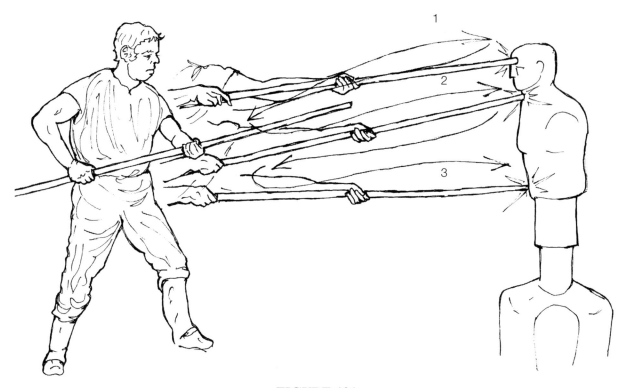

FIGURE 121

Action 2: On completion of the third thrust, execute a hand change while moving the opposite leg to the lead and repeat Action 1.

NOTE: Practice Actions 1 and 2 as a complete set 10–15 times until you become proficient.

Action 3: This time you will execute a hand change after each thrust, shifting your targets to the opponent's opposite side. Simply, execute a two-handed thrust to the left side of the opponent's head, make a hand change, and execute a second thrust to the right side of the opponent's head. Repeat this process through all the same targets engaged in Actions 1 and 2.

NOTE: Make all your thrusts fast and violent, not unlike that of a snake striking. Remember that the thrust is a very effective disruption technique that completely halts an opponent's forward momentum.

TRAINING OBJECTIVE 14

Task: Execute single-handed thrusts into four primary target areas.

Condition: You need a staff and training area sufficient to accommodate 360-degree movement and overhead strikes with the weapon. You may use a heavy bag, silhouette target, or padded pell.

Standard: The purpose of this drill is to improve proficiency in executing the one-handed thrust from middle-guard positions.

Action 1: Assume a middle-guard position within striking range of the opponent target, as depicted in Figure 122. Shift your rear hand to the point of balance for a single-handed thrust (as illustrated in Figure 116, page 101). As soon as the balance point is achieved, step off line to the left while driving the tip of the staff around in an ascending arc that curves to strike the opponent's left eye. Figure 123 depicts this

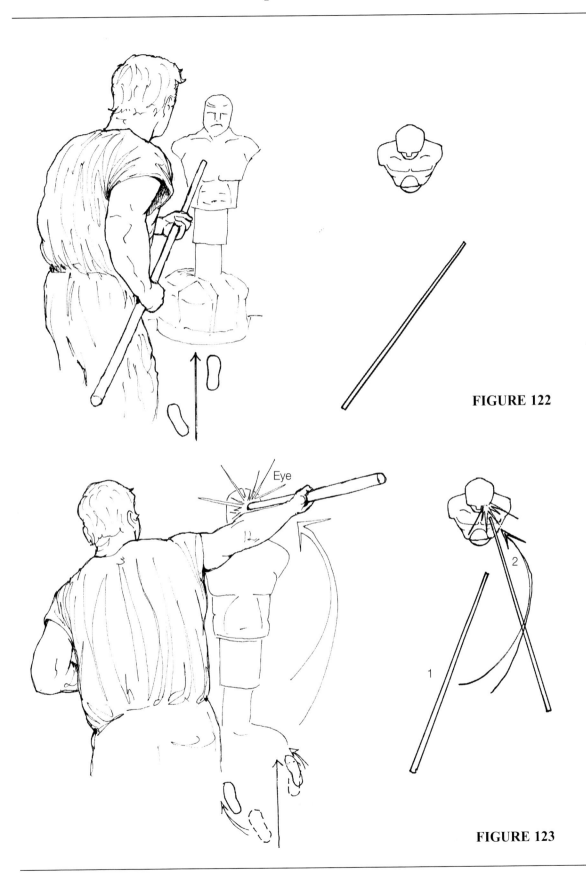

FIGURE 122

Eye

1

2

FIGURE 123

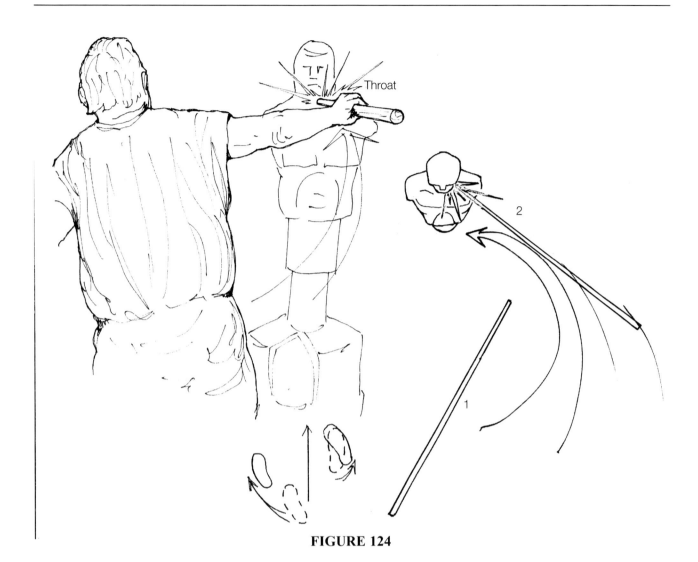

Throat

2

1

FIGURE 124

action from behind and overhead. On impact immediately, pull the staff back and return to the middle guard.

Action 2: Repeat Action 1, only this time target the opponent's throat and then return again to the middle guard. This technique is illustrated in Figure 124.

Action 3: Repeat Action 1 but target the opponent's ribs, as illustrated in Figure 125. Again return to the middle-guard position.

Action 4: This time instead of executing the arcing thrust described in Actions 1–3,

push the tip of the spear forward and upward into the opponent's groin area, as depicted in Figure 126. Note that the footwork for this thrust requires you to slide forward slightly, remaining in line with the target.

Action 5: As with Training Objective 13, change hands, move the opposite leg forward, and repeat this exercise with the left hand.

NOTE: Repeat this objective 10 to 15 times until you are proficient.

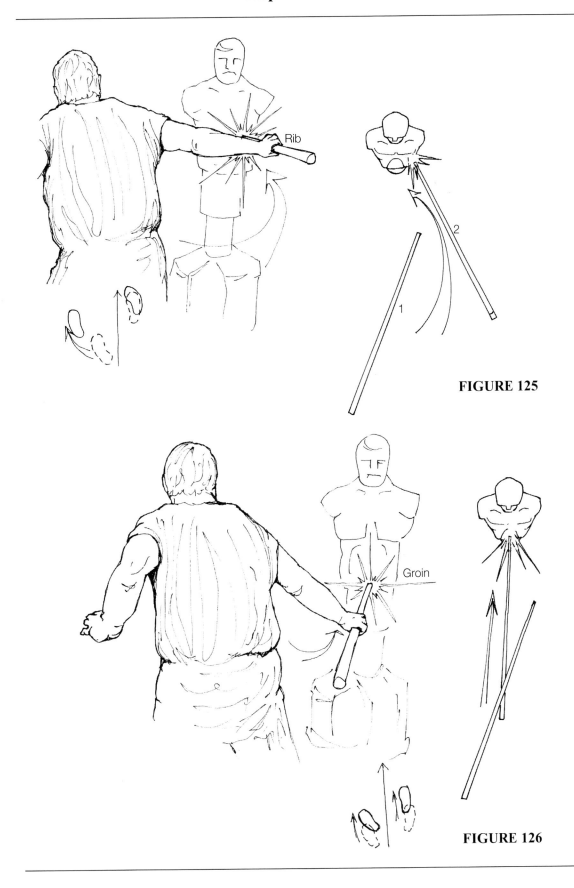

Rib

FIGURE 125

Groin

FIGURE 126

CHAPTER 11
ASPECTS OF THE BLOCK

The bottom line for any fight with weapons is that there will come a time when it is going to be necessary to stop an incoming strike or thrust. You may have been caught off guard and need to impede or divert the opponent's weapon to keep from getting hit. You may want to stop an opponent's movement to get yourself in position to deliver an attack of your own. Both of these situations require you to use the structural strength of the weapon and your body to halt the attacking movement.

Most of the time a block will require you to stay inside the box momentarily. Regardless of whether a particular technique or style places emphasis on deflecting or parrying, you need to know how to block with your weapon just in case those wonderful techniques don't work and you end up on the receiving end of an attack.

There are basically four common blocks that can be used with most of the grips and motions depicted in Figures 29 and 30 (pages 31–32): high, low, left and right, and Fiore's. For simplicity's sake, I will use the middle-guard and hand positions shown earlier in Figure 10 (page 8) to illustrate the blocking techniques. I am going to address the blocks within the sequence contained in Figures 127 and 128. This will serve as a basis for a drill to be performed later.

HIGH BLOCK

This block positions the staff horizontally to address strikes that your opponent may deliver into the Angle 1, 2, and 8 target areas (depicted earlier in Figure 35 on page 36). Usually these high-angle attacks will target the head, neck, or shoulders. Execute the block by pushing the staff violently upward with the arms slightly flexed, as depicted in Figure 127A.

The opponent's strike is usually received in the center of the staff in the approximate location of the second quarter. But this is not an absolute, as you might have to shift the hands either left or right to accommodate the blow and prevent it from impacting on the hands. You can also receive the blow in the areas outside the hands, roughly in the first and third quarters, but keep in mind that these actions may require a slight angling of the staff into the strike to provide adequate leverage. While the footwork and body motions for this block may be forward or backward, it is generally recommended to step or slide into the incoming strike in order to put one's body weight and strength into stopping the blow. It is very important to keep the wrist and forearms in line; otherwise, the strike will "blow" right through the block. It is best to think of all blocks as

FIGURE 127A

FIGURE 127B

being offensively powerful and disruptive to the opponent's intent. Remember that this and all blocks should be considered momentary pauses prior to launching a violent counterattack.

LOW BLOCK

Figure 127B depicts the execution of a low block immediately following a high block. In this case the staff is pulled forcefully downward to halt attacks into Angle 5, 6, and 7 target areas. While the high block is pressed upward, not unlike a bench press with a barbell, the low block uses a pulling action that arcs the staff down and into the incoming attack. Again, the wrist and forearms should move

into a line on impact, creating a violent striking effect. The body motion requires that the threatened leg be passed backward on initiation of the block. The "feel" for this action is not unlike that of pulling an open window closed. Note that this block can be used to stop incoming thrusts more effectively than the high block.

NOTE: Take a close look at Figure 127A and then rapidly shift your eyes to 127 B. Focus first on the action of the arms and then the legs while rapidly shifting the eyes back and forth between the two illustrations. Note how as you do this, the drawings seem to move, giving you a feel for the blocking action and the sequential drill (discussed later).

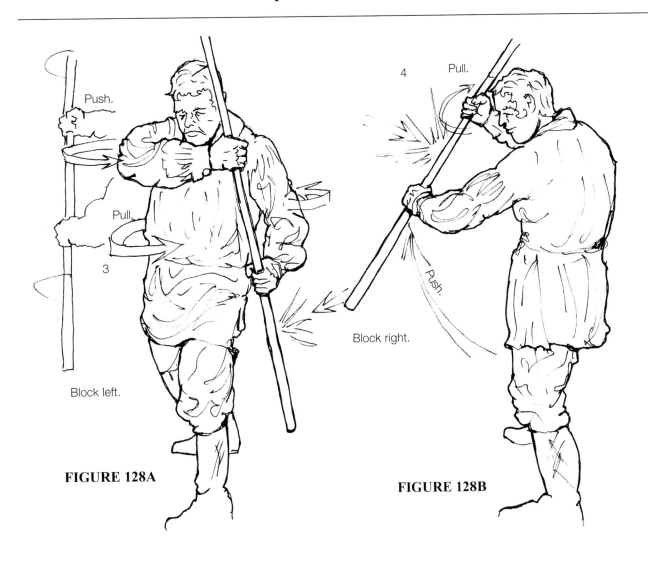

Push.

Pull.

3

Block left.

FIGURE 128A

4

Pull.

Push.

Block right.

FIGURE 128B

LEFT AND RIGHT BLOCKS

For those attacks that come into Angle 3 and 4 target areas, you have the vertical left and right blocks. As with the high and low blocks, the positions of the hands and the part of the staff receiving the strike may vary, depending on your position and that of your opponent. Figure 128A depicts a left block while Figure 128B illustrates the block to your right.

This block should be thought of as "slamming a door closed to prevent entry." The strike is executed while holding the staff vertically or at slight angle with the heel forward. The staff may be held tight against the body or approximately 12 inches out with the arms in a half-chamber position, as seen in

Figure 128A. The action of the block requires a push-pull action with the left or right hand, depending on whether the block is to the left or right, as A and B. To fully support this block it is best to pivot the hip into the incoming strike and bend slightly to compress into a more grounded stance. Note that these vertical blocks can be used effectively against thrusts as well.

NOTE: As with the note for the high/low blocks, focus on Figures 128A and B and shift your eyes rapidly back and forth between to get a feel for the motion of this blocking sequence. Once you have accomplished this, lay both Figures 127A and B and 128A and B on a table side by side. Beginning with 127A, rapidly shift your eyes from left to right, ending with 128B. Go back to the first illustration and repeat the process until you begin to "see" the sequence and get a feel for the movement pattern.

TRAINING OBJECTIVE 15

Task: Execute the blocking sequence depicted in Figures 127 and 128.

Condition: You need a staff and training area sufficient to accommodate 360-degree movement and overhead strikes with the weapon. You might consider doing this exercise in front of a mirror initially to examine your execution of each move. For this objective, you will be executing this sequence in the open air, simulating reaction to incoming attacks. Later you will use this same sequence to practice your blocking techniques with an armed training partner delivering strikes.

Standard:

Action 1: Visualize yourself facing an opponent armed with a staff and delivering an Angle 8 attack to your head. Immediately slide forward, driving your staff upward and receiving the blow in the center of your staff as depicted in Figure 127A.

Action 2: Suddenly your opponent strikes upward with the heel of his staff into your groin with an Angle 7 attack. Immediately you pull your staff down in the fashion depicted in Figure 127B and block the incoming blow.

Action 3: Visualize your opponent shifting back and to your left and delivering an Angle 3 strike to your arm. Immediately execute a block left, as depicted in Figure 128A.

Action 4: Visualize your opponent sliding closer and to your right while delivering an Angle 4 strike to your hip. Immediately execute a block right, as depicted in Figure 128B.

NOTE: Repeat this sequence 10–15 times until you are proficient. As you become comfortable with the blocks, begin to experiment with the various types of footwork movements discussed earlier, focusing on moving outside the box after each block.

FIORE'S BLOCK

"This way I wait with dagger and the staff: The staff will protect, the dagger will hit your chest; And what I do with the staff I would do with the sword, Although the sword would be stronger."
—Fiore dei Liberi, 1410

The medieval fight master Fiore dei Liberi did not directly address many techniques for the staff in his historical manuscript *Flos Duellatorum*. Rather, he equated its use as being very similar to that of the sword and provided only minimum coverage by including it in the section on spear techniques. In one of the few dedicated techniques for the staff, dei Liberi depicted the butt of the staff grounded in front of the lead leg and used more or less as a shield to defend against attacks by swinging it left or right, as I have re-created in Figure 129A. Figure 129B is my rendering from Fiore's manuscript where this technique is used in combination with the dagger. One of the advantages of this block that caught my attention was the almost complete protection that it offers for high-, middle-, and low-line attacks. You might say that you are sort of "hiding behind the tree" for protection. You'll see this used later in the engagement scenarios, but for now experiment with it and incorporate it at the end of the blocking sequence addressed in Training Objective 15.

FIGURE 129A

FIGURE 129B

CHAPTER 12
ASPECTS OF DEFLECTING

If studying the sword, you might refer to this technique as *parrying*. The technique generally involves pushing, tapping, or even striking an opponent's incoming strike, taking it off its original trajectory.

Deflecting is usually associated with some sort of body or footwork that moves you out of the way and presents an immediate opening to counterattack your opponent. Deflections tend to focus weapon on weapon but can be directed to hand, joint, or muscle targets on the arm as a form of disruption technique. Figure 130 presents an example of a common deflection.

There are basically three types of deflection techniques: horizontal, vertical, and circular.

HORIZONTAL DEFLECTION

This technique involves moving the staff to either the left or right side of the body (usually with an associated hand change) and holding it almost parallel to the horizon. The

FIGURE 130

opponent's weapon is deflected to the side with a pulling action. This technique can be used against incoming thrusts or strikes at the high-, middle-, and low-line areas. Depending on the angle, it may be necessary to drop the tip of the staff slightly; in the case of some low-line attacks, the tip may almost touch the ground.

Let's get more familiar with the horizontal deflection through the following training objective.

TRAINING OBJECTIVE 16

Task: Execute horizontal deflections against attacks coming in at the high-, middle-, and low-line areas.

Condition: You need a staff and a training area sufficient to accommodate 360-degree movement and overhead strikes with the weapon. You might consider doing this exercise in front of a mirror initially to examine the execution of each move. For this objective, you will be executing this sequence in the open air, simulating reaction to incoming attacks. Later you will use this same sequence to exercise your blocking techniques with an armed training partner delivering strikes.

Standard:

  Action 1: Take up a middle-guard position in the training area. Visualize your opponent facing you in a middle-guard position. Suddenly he executes an Angle 1 strike at your neck, similar to that illustrated in Figure 131. Violently pull your staff up to the horizontal position, similar to that in Figure 132, and simultaneously swing your left leg back and pivot on the right foot. You should receive the strike on either the fourth or third quarter while the arms shift to the rear. It may be necessary to lift the heel of the staff, depending on the angle of the incoming attack. Immediately return to the middle-guard position.

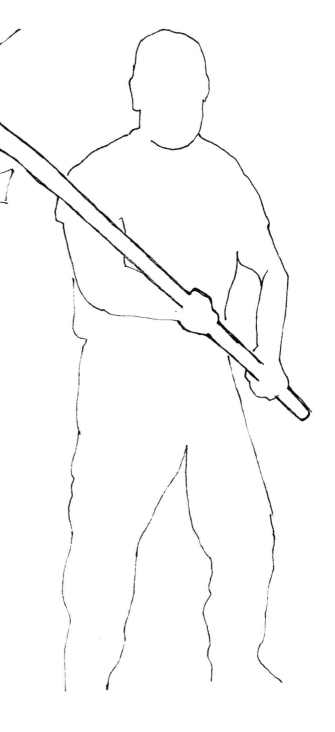

FIGURE 131

FIGURE 132

Action 2: Visualize your opponent attacking with an Angle 4 strike to your left hip, similar to that indicated in Figure 133. While maintaining your staff at the level of the middle guard, pull the staff back along the line of your waist. Simultaneously slide backward while pivoting the hips and left leg around to the left rear as depicted in Figure 134. In this case remember that it may be necessary to lift the heel of the staff and drop the tip in order to strike the opponent's weapon. Immediately return to the middle-guard position.

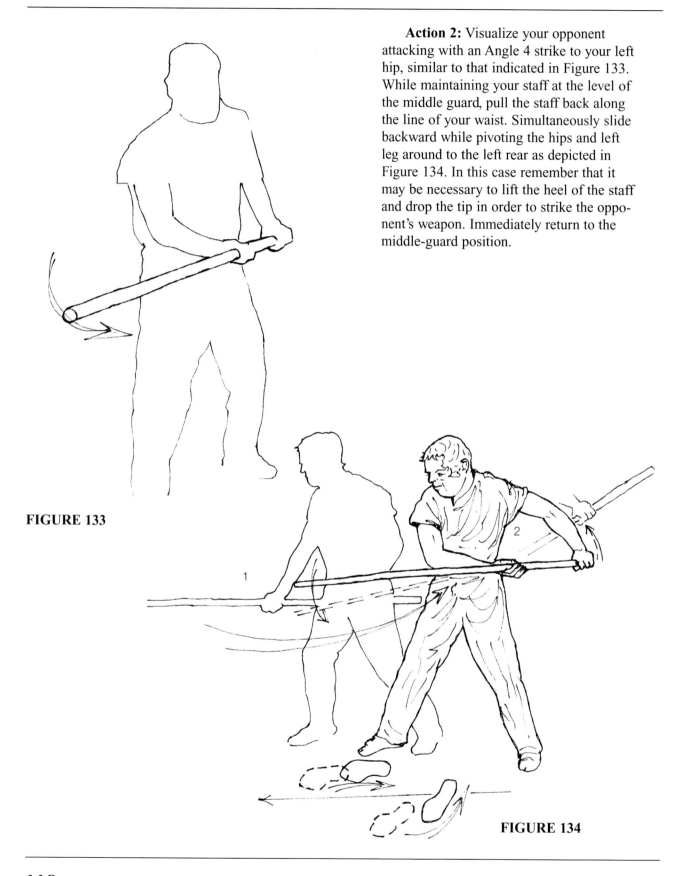

FIGURE 133

FIGURE 134

Action 3: Visualize your opponent executing an ascending attack toward your rear leg, similar to that indicated in Figure 135. On your opponent's cue, drop the tip of the staff while swinging the left leg back to the left rear and pivoting on the right foot, as indicated in Figure 136. Again, remember that you may need to raise the tip of the staff, depending on the height of the opponent's strike above the ground.

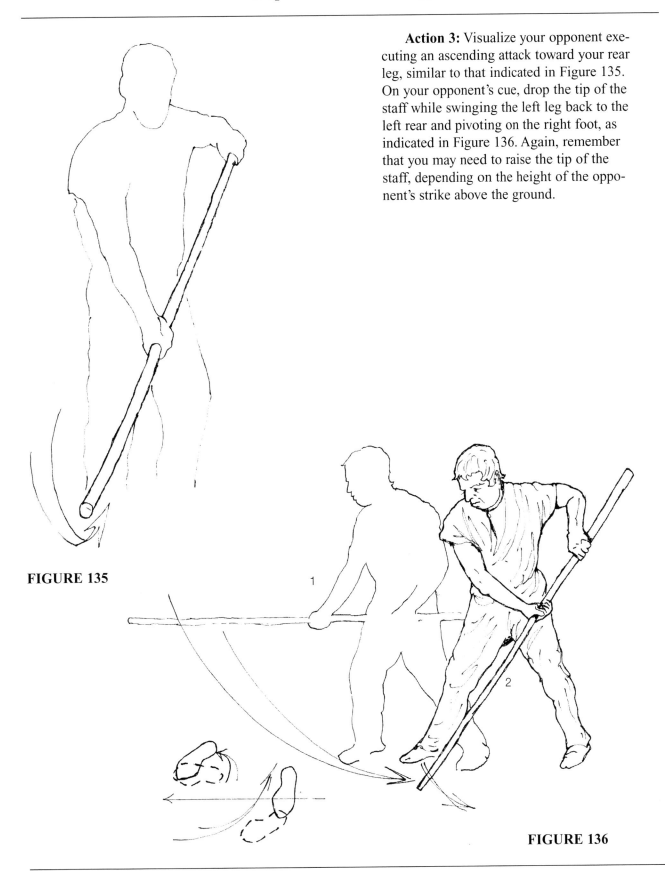

FIGURE 135

FIGURE 136

Action 4: Change hands while moving to a middle-guard position with the left leg forward and repeat Actions 1–3 from the opposite side.

NOTE: Repeat this sequence 10–15 times until you are proficient. As you become comfortable with the actions, begin to experiment with the various types of footwork discussed earlier, focusing on moving outside the box after each deflection.

VERTICAL DEFLECTION

This technique involves deflecting with the tip or the heel pointed skyward. Normally the staff is held close to the body with the upper portion at roughly a 20-degree angle from the body similar to that shown in Figure 137. Incoming strikes are received on the fourth, third, or first quarter of the staff, depending on whether the heel or tip is pointed skyward. The feel for this deflection is similar to that for a forceful strike used to deflect the opponent's weapon; execute an immediate follow-up as the weapon is displaced. Let's examine this further in the following training objective.

TRAINING OBJECTIVE 17

Task: Execute vertical deflections against attacks coming in at the high-, middle-, and low-line areas.

Condition: You need a staff and training area sufficient to accommodate 360-degree movement and overhead strikes with the weapon. You might consider doing this exercise in front of a mirror initially to examine your execution of each move. For this objective, you will be executing this sequence in the open air, simulating reac-

tion to incoming attacks. Later you will use this same sequence with an armed training partner delivering strikes.

Standard:

Action 1: Take up a middle-guard position and visualize an opponent delivering an Angle 1 strike to your neck. Immediately pull the staff across your body violently to your left, with the tip pointed upward as in Figure 137. If your opponent is very close, you might have to hold the staff almost vertical, similar to that illustrated in the blocks in Figures 128A and B. It is desirable to receive the impact of the strike between the fourth and third quarters, knocking it off to the left as you swing your left leg around, as illustrated in Figure 137.

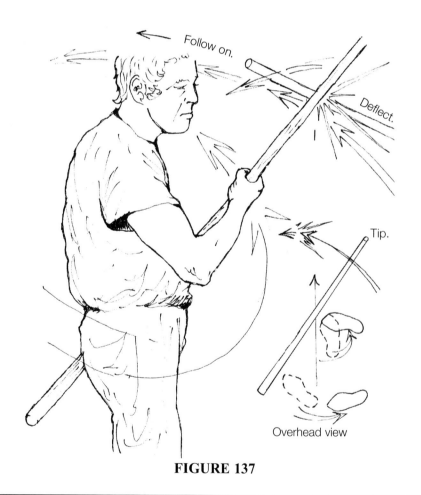

FIGURE 137

Action 2: Visualize your opponent executing an Angle 2 attack to your neck with the heel of his staff leading. As you sense the incoming strike, push the heel of your staff up and around, deflecting the opponent's strike to your right. As you initiate the deflection, shift your torso to the right and step forward with the left foot while pivoting on the right foot. Figure 138 depicts this action.

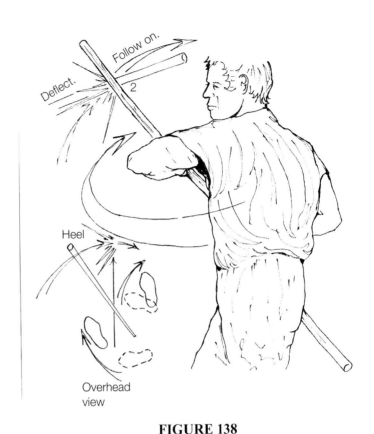

FIGURE 138

FIGURE 139

Action 3: Visualize your opponent striking at your ribs with an Angle 3 attack. Immediately pull the butt of the staff upward while pushing the third quarter of the staff into your opponent's weapon and deflecting it to your left, as depicted in Figure 139.

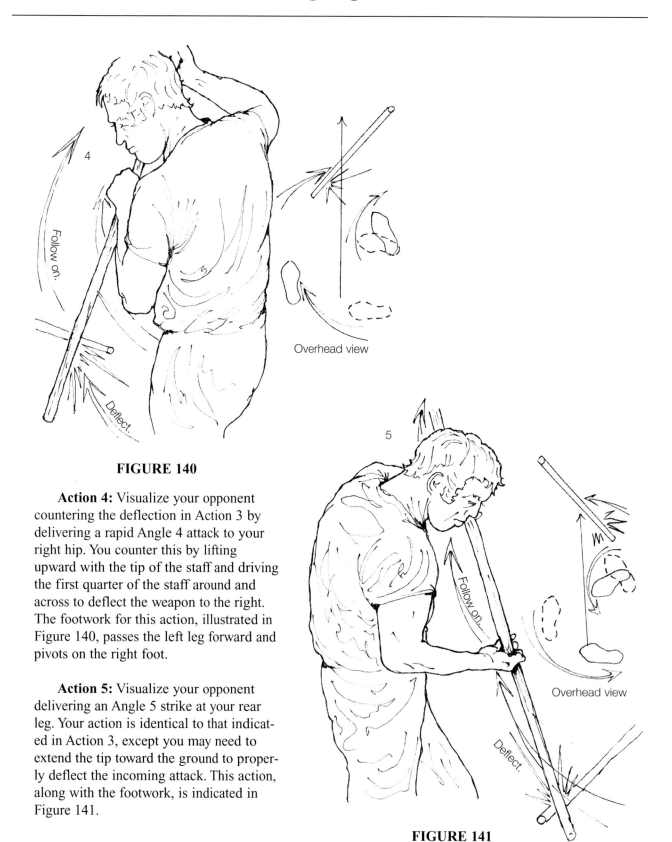

FIGURE 140

Overhead view

Follow on.

Deflect.

Action 4: Visualize your opponent countering the deflection in Action 3 by delivering a rapid Angle 4 attack to your right hip. You counter this by lifting upward with the tip of the staff and driving the first quarter of the staff around and across to deflect the weapon to the right. The footwork for this action, illustrated in Figure 140, passes the left leg forward and pivots on the right foot.

Action 5: Visualize your opponent delivering an Angle 5 strike at your rear leg. Your action is identical to that indicated in Action 3, except you may need to extend the tip toward the ground to properly deflect the incoming attack. This action, along with the footwork, is indicated in Figure 141.

Overhead view

Follow on.

Deflect.

FIGURE 141

6

Follow on.

Deflect.

Overhead view

FIGURE 142

Action 6: Visualize your opponent delivering an Angle 6 attack to your lead leg. Your action is identical to that indicated in Action 4, except you may need to extend the heel toward the ground to properly deflect the incoming attack. This action, along with the footwork, is indicated in Figure 142.

NOTE: After you have experimented with the execution of each of the actions for this objective, execute them together as one flowing sequence. Repeat this 10 to 15 times until you are proficient.

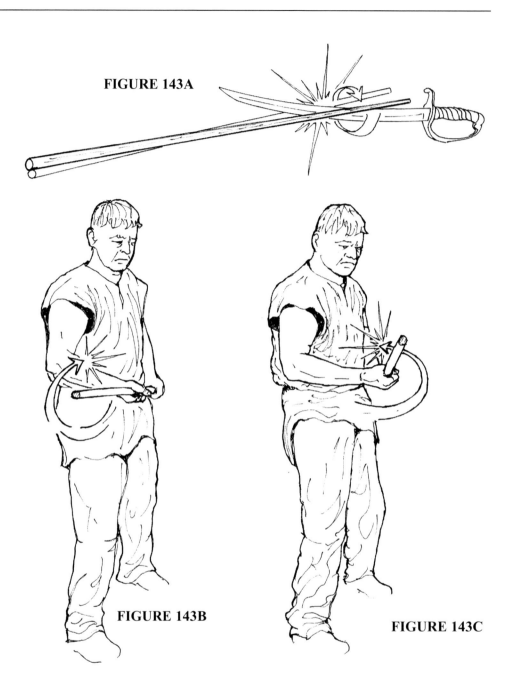

FIGURE 143A

FIGURE 143B

FIGURE 143C

CIRCULAR DEFLECTION

I have heard it said that the Chinese referred to this technique as "Dragon whips his tail." I don't know if that is exactly correct, but it is as good a memory jogger as the next. Basically, this deflection begins with you moving within striking range of your opponent's weapon, anywhere between the tip and middle portion of the weapon. You can gently touch his weapon to "sense" that you're within range or simply move directly into the deflection. Personally, I like to give his weapon a slight tap just prior to execution. This deflection is executed by circling the tip or third quarter of the staff in a tight arc around the opponent's weapon and then violently striking it from the opposite side, diverting the weapon away and off line. Usually this will create an opening for a strike or thrust. Figure 143A depicts this action from the side while 143B and C demonstrate the deflection going in either direction.

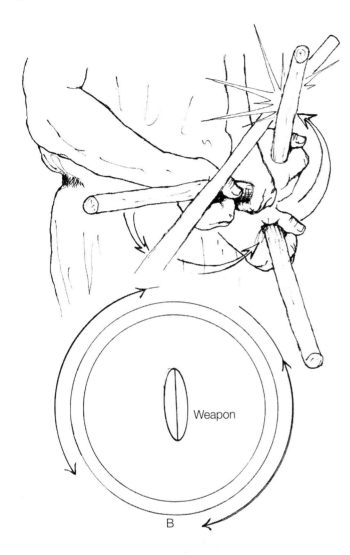

FIGURE 144A

Weapon

B

FIGURE 144B

Figure 144A further clarifies the nature of this deflection, with particular emphasis on how tight the circle should be. The diagram in Figure 144B is technically very close to the actual size of the circle that the fourth quarter of the staff makes to either the left or right. Figure 145 gives a user's view of a circular deflection to your right followed by an immediate strike to the opponent's hands. Note that openings are also there for a thrust to the opponent's abdomen, throat, or eye. The opportunity to execute a short strike to the opponent's head is also available.

FIGURE 145

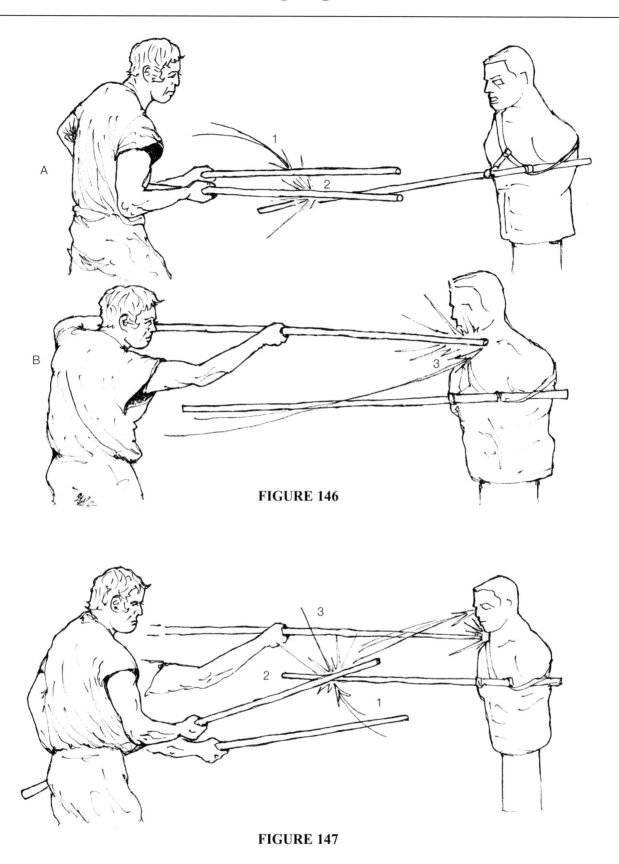

FIGURE 146

FIGURE 147

BASIC BEAT

The same tapping motion can also be used without the circular motion by just moving directly into the opponent's weapon from the top (Figure 146) or either the left or right side (Figure 147) and following on with a short strike or thrust.

TACTICAL NOTE: The circular deflection and basic beat are best suited just as the opponent's weapon comes into striking range. The action should be violent and fast, moving directly into the attack. If you pause between the deflection and attack, the opponent will have time to counter or launch his own attack.

TRAINING OBJECTIVE 18

Task: Execute circular and the basic beat deflection techniques.

Condition: You need a staff and training area sufficient to accommodate 360-degree movement and overhead strikes with the weapon. Remember the two-hand targets depicted in Figures 79–84 (pages 73–76) and the exercises you did for Training Objective 7? You will use these as striking targets to simulate your opponent's weapon and head to become used to full-force circular and basic beat deflection. You will also need a silhouette target with a staff attached, similar to that in Figure 65 (page 62).

Standard:

Action 1: Have your training partner take up a position within striking distance and hold the targets, as indicated in Figure 148. Take up a middle-guard position with the right leg forward. Practice executing the circular deflection technique at slow speed until you are comfortable with it. Focus on making the circular movement in a very tight circle, followed by a violent twist of the wrist of the lead hand, which snaps the fourth quarter of the staff into the target. Repeat this, gradually increasing to medium and then full speed. Note how the target is diverted off the centerline, revealing openings for short strikes and thrusts.

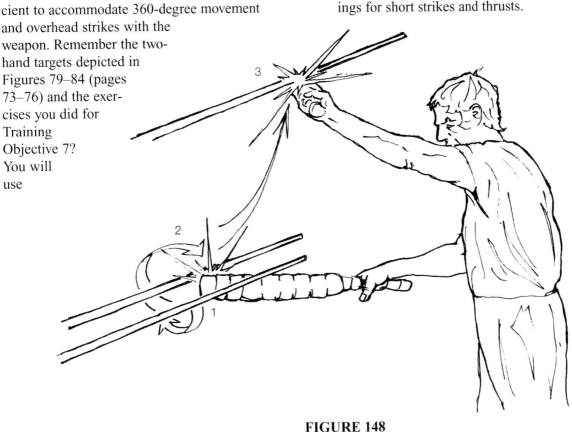

FIGURE 148

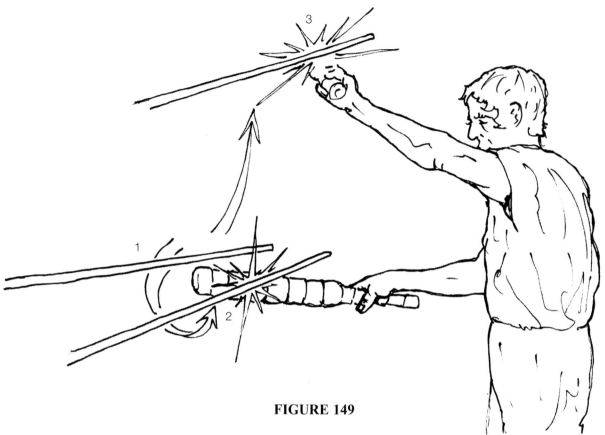

FIGURE 149

Action 2: Again moving at slow speed, execute the circular deflection technique to the left and then immediately follow with a short strike to your partner's hand target as depicted in Figure 148. Repeat this action with a circular deflection to the right followed by the short strike depicted in Figure 149. Repeat this action, gradually increasing to full speed.

Action 3: If you do not have a training partner you can attach a staff to the silhouette target similar to that depicted in Figure 65 (page 62) and repeat the actions of the training objective until you are proficient.

NOTE: This exercise should become part of your regular training regimen with the staff. You should experiment frequently with a variety of follow-on strikes, including thrusts and long and short strikes at a variety of high- and midline targets. Be sure to practice moving to new positions on the left

and right of your opponent immediately after the circular deflection or the follow-on attack.

TRAINING OBJECTIVE 19

Task: Execute circular and the basic beat deflection techniques against a training partner armed with a staff. Include movement and footwork to change position during the execution of the techniques.

Condition: You need a staff and training area sufficient to accommodate 360-degree movement and overhead strikes with the weapon. During this exercise, you will be working with a training partner armed with a staff. You will be executing the circular deflection and basic techniques while you move toward your opponent and your opponent moves toward you. You will be executing the deflections at full speed against your partner's staff and then, as you move, look-

FIGURE 150

ing for target openings created by the deflection. The idea here is only to "see" the target openings; do *not* execute any follow-on strikes.

Standard:

Action 1: Take up a middle-guard position approximately 2–3 feet from your training partner, who is in the same middle guard. In this action, your partner will not be moving; rather he will be serving as a static target for you. Using the step-forward technique discussed earlier, advance toward your training partner until you are in striking range to execute the circular deflection against the fourth or third quarter of his staff. Your last forward step should bring you into this position.

Action 2: As soon as you arrive in position, execute a circular deflection to the left. Immediately on impact, move to the right

and look for target opportunities. Again be careful to avoid striking your training partner. Once you have completed this action, move back to the middle-guard position and signal your partner that it is his turn to practice the technique while you serve as the static target. Exercise this rotating sequence at least 15 times until both of you are satisfied with the results.

Action 3: Repeat the sequence in Action 2 using a circular deflection to the right. This time move to the right on impact.

Action 4: This time you repeat Actions 2 and 3, except you remain static while your training partner moves toward you into range. As soon as his weapon comes into range, execute the technique and step left or right as appropriate.

Figure 150 provides a conceptual visualization of this objective.

CHAPTER 13
SOME CONCEPTUAL THOUGHTS ON THE STAFF

This is probably as good a place as any to pause and discuss some more of the conceptual aspects for using the staff as a weapon. You might say we will be talking about the *language* of training and fighting with the staff. This is more than just technical information; rather, it is a way of developing and understanding the many elements of fighting. I was told once that these concepts seem to run like a thread through all my manuals, and I see no reason why they are not related to the staff. In fact, they can be related to all weapons.

> "Then your hand will strike sponta-
> neously out of emptiness, with speed and
> power, without taking note of the starting
> point of the movement."
> —Miyamoto Musashi, 1645

My martial studies have led me to two conceptual tenets that apply to most combative situations. These are nothing new—historians, martial artists, and warriors have been talking and writing about them for ages, using a variety of terms to describe them. The tenets used here are not necessarily historical, but rather a mixed bag that includes modern ones as well. This is my take on them:

1. Everything is a matter of distance, time, and position.
2. Read the messages of the opponent, weapon, environment, and mind.

EVERYTHING IS A MATTER OF DISTANCE, TIME, AND POSITION

Circle of the Mind

Over the years it has been my pleasure to train with Maestros Jeanette and Ramon Martinez in the Spanish system of fencing called *La Verdadera Destreza.* This unique husband-and-wife team is responsible for teaching me how to apply Girard Thibault's 1630 publication *Academy of the Sword* and the Spanish Circle to all the weapons taught in my curriculum. You will see this in *Bowie and Big Knife Fighting System, Advanced Bowie Techniques, The Fighting Tomahawk,* and *The Fighting Sword.* Years after writing those books, I still find myself amazed at the adaptability of this circular training aid to almost any weapon.

I am also honored to have trained with Maestro de Armas Blancas Sevillanas James Loriega. From him I learned another application of the circle that is found in the 19th-century *Manual of the Baratero* by Mariano de Rementeria y Fica (details of the application can be found in Maestro Loriega's translation of *Manual of the Baratero,* available from Paladin Press). This is probably the oldest dedicated manual on the subject of knife fighting and is unique in that it describes a fighting tactic called the *corrida,* which seems to have been influenced by the Spanish Circle.

While the Spanish fencing places the circle in front of the fighter with the opponent in the center, the corrida describes an imaginary circle around each of the combatants. In short, each combatant has his own circle that moves with him throughout the course of the fight. Since this term actually describes a tactic, the term *terreno*, meaning boundary, might also be used to describe this circle. The corrida involves moving to one side or another in the same guard position. This is done to acquire target opportunities or lure the opponent into making an attack into the terreno and thus come into range.

During my experimentation, I found the corrida tactic to be more suited to two-handed weapons, such as the staff, than the tactic found in the Spanish Circle, which was designed exclusively for single-handed use of the sword. Consequently, I've included the terreno in this manual as a visual aid to both presenting the various techniques and "seeing" the applications of time, distance, and position. Remember, this is an imaginary circle that functions as a conceptual guide; it is not a technique in itself. Now let's take a look at the application of this circular concept to the staff.

Determining the Circle

Visualize the terreno, or boundary, as an imaginary circle around both you and your opponent(s). The maximum range or length of your weapon determines the circumference and diameter. You are positioned in the center, and the circle moves with both you and your opponent. Figure 151 presents an overhead diagram of this circle, which you will use from time to

time throughout this text to illustrate the relationship of the attacker to the defender when executing specific techniques.

The footprints in the center indicate your position in one of the basic guards (in this case the middle). The footprints stand astride a line with an arrow on one end to indicate the general direction you are facing or where your opponent is initially located. Radiating out from the center are eight lines that terminate at the far circle. These are simply points of reference to determine angles of attack/defense and target opportunities created by the circular movement. Don't get "buried" in the mathematical aspects or the precision of position. Remember, this is simply a guide to teach a concept. Note the staff drawing adjacent to the footprints. This is an approximate for a 6-foot staff held in the middle-guard position (illustrated in Figure 10 on page 8). The dashed line extending from the tip of that staff indicates this guard when held with the long grip.

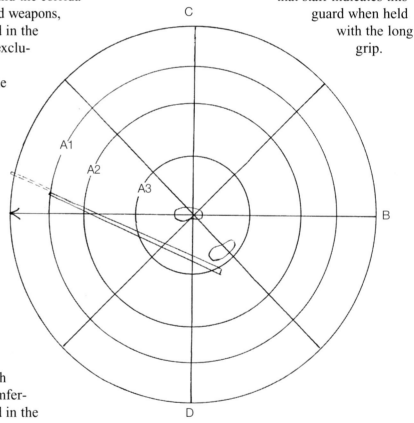

FIGURE 151

Now let's engage in a bit of mental gymnastics to determine how the aspects of distance, time, and position apply to this circle. *Remember, this is your circle.* It is imaginary and moving with you. It is a thought process imprinted on the mind's eye to guide you to those openings inside and outside the box. Think about it.

Aspect of Distance

At this point you need to physically draw the circle on the ground or floor wherever you train. If you are on a concrete slab, you may want to use chalk, a nonpermanent marker, or masking tape to lay out the circle. I saw a demonstration of this done on the beach one time and another with the line-marking powder used on football fields. Remember, this is a training aid, and you'll only need to actually draw it once or twice to get it imprinted on your mind. I have this circle painted on the concrete slab of my garage training hall. When I was using jigsaw mats, it was painted on those. If you are an instructor with lots of students, you will find that this works well as a training aid. It is particularly useful during full-speed sparring when you stop the action and indicate to the students their position and why this or that technique did or did not work.

Take up a middle-guard position. Note where your lead foot is and mark it on the surface. Grip the staff with a long grip and extend your arms as indicated in Figure 152. Squat down and lay the staff on the ground with the tip pointing in the same direction as your lead foot. Place your trailing hand on the heel of the staff where it touches your big toe. Leaving the staff in place, draw a line along the length of the staff on the surface, adding an arrow where the tip is. Now take the staff and place the heel of the staff in the position where the heel of your lead foot was and draw a line along its length as you did before. This will form line A through B indicated in Figure 151.

At this time, have a partner take a piece of cord whose length runs from your lead foot to the end of the line. While you hold the line tight at the lead-foot position, have your partner swing an arc 360 degrees, scribing a circle on the surface. This is your maximum range line based on the length of your weapon and extension of your arms. This will accommodate both strikes and two-handed thrusts using the long grip.

Take a look at Figure 152 and note the relationship between you and the length of the weapon as it relates to the range to the target. This is your guide for fighting at long range with your staff and body type. Take a moment and study this. Take up a position in the middle guard in the center while your partner stands with his lead foot on the end of line A. Pick up your staff and extend it toward your partner. Have your partner reach forward and touch your staff. Feel the distance and think about where you and your partner have to be to initiate an attack. This is what the military calls *range determination*, and it is extremely important when you decide to fight using long-range techniques. For example, if your opponent has a shorter weapon, this could

Aspects of Distance

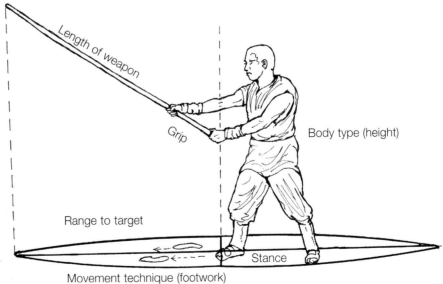

FIGURE 152

become a very critical factor. Another point to remember is how a certain object in the environment can help you determine range. Take the staff and extend it in the long grip discussed earlier. Go up to a tree, curb, or any object, and extend the tip until it touches that object. Note how the tree and distance look. Do this several times until you have the distance between you and the A line firmly imprinted on your mind.

Now that you have the center of this line determined, lay the staff down and repeat the drawing process for lines C through D, as well as the other corresponding lines that make up the circumference of your circle.

As you work with this circle more, you will find that you use only 180 degrees of the circle from the direction you face. This is fine for dealing only with single opponents, but remember when you face multiple opponents your ability to visualize 360 degrees is critical. If the opponent to your front is out of range and the opponent to your left has stepped inside your circle, you might want to address him first or execute a move that changes this relationship. Take quite a bit of time to work with a partner measuring this long-range circle. Practice a few slow-speed thrusts and note how quickly it covers the distance in comparison to a strike. Give some thought to what targets would be available first at this range. Experiment with both high and low guards and see how they impact on your ability to engage at long range. A good example is a high or low guard, which more or less mandates that you execute either ascending or descending strikes if you are to engage on this outer ring of the circle.

So far our equation has examined the length of the weapon, the grip, and the stance as it relates to the range to target. The final consideration is your body type. Bottom line: you must take into account your height and the length of your arms. The ability to attack at long range for one person may not necessarily be so for another.

Now let's look as some other aspects of our circle in terms of determining distance or range. Looking back at Figure 151 you will see that there are three other concentric circles indicated as A1 through A3. These represent the range lines for a 6-foot staff held

in the middle guard position in Figure 10. Note that we are not using the long grip here but a mixed grip with the trail hand approximately 12 to 15 inches from the heel of the staff. This makes for difference in range that you have to be aware of. The circle at A1 indicates the staff is held straight and level at the horizontal. The circle at A2 reflects the range in the high guard depicted earlier in Figure 11. Those instances where the high guard positions the staff above the head were not included since they are essentially the same as A2 during a strike from that position. The circle at A3 indicates the range when the staff is pulled back against the chest with arms chambered. This is the really close-engagement area. Once more, do not think of these circles as absolutes; these ranges are approximate and vary according to what you are doing during an engagement. They are nothing more than a method of range-distance determination. Don't get hung up on geometric precision here—you are thinking conceptually.

The following exercise will help to reinforce this and get these ranges imprinted on your mind. Have your training partner assume a middle-guard position opposite you. Take up the long grip and extend your arms and staff as shown in Figure 152 earlier. Bring both staffs down to the horizontal and adjust the distance until both tips are touching. On command, immediately change from the long grip to the mixed grip discussed for Figure 153. Keep your staffs horizontal, with both tips reasonably in line. Notice the space between you and your partner. Be aware of its relationship to your partner's lead foot. This is a mental cue that neither of you is in range. Now, have your partner change back to the long grip, but this time he does not extend his arms. Note that while your tips are not touching, the space is not that great. In fact, your partner can hit your staff with a simple extension of his arms. Note that with the basic beat technique your partner could move your staff and be within range to deliver a short strike to your hand. Both you and your partner should experiment a lot with the approach just covered, with the idea of imprinting in your mind exactly what things look like at this range. Repeat this procedure using the ranges for A2 and A3, focusing on being able to estimate the range of your opponent with the weapon held in those various positions.

FIGURE 153

Practice moving though the various positions by moving in a circle while still maintaining the range. After you are comfortable with this, experiment with changing the range by stepping forward while your partner steps back to maintain the range. You'll want to devote at least 15 minutes each session to practice this approach until you have the distances firmly imprinted on your mind.

You should also try this under conditions where light is limited. Practice range estimation on the side of hills, inside buildings, and on both rough and smooth terrain. You will find that if you practice this on a beach or in sand, your footprints will leave some key indicators that are also helpful. Remember,

the goal here is to be able to tell immediately whether your opponent's actions have placed him in position to attack and vice versa. Study this a lot.

Aspect of Time

Another aspect that is tied directly to distance is that of time. This aspect focuses on the character of the weapon and the associated movement of both you and your opponent. But this explanation is really simplistic in that it deals with how quick one can get in range and attack or get the hell out of the way to keep from being hit. In Figure 154 you can see how the length of the weapon and the technique being used have a direct impact on how efficient an

Aspects of Time

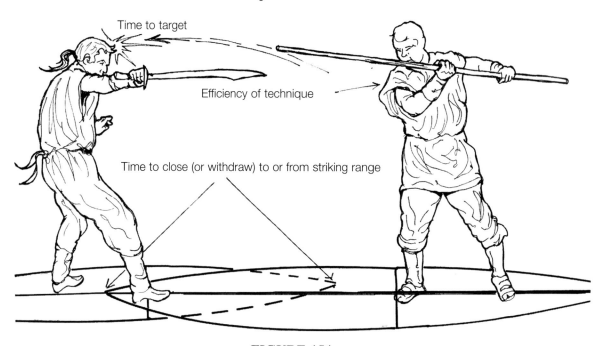

FIGURE 154

attack or defense will be. Factors such as the delivery speed of a thrust versus that of a cut are key considerations once the range has been closed. The time it takes to move from one point to another during delivery of the technique also must play into a fighting tactic. In Figure 154 it is pretty clear that the length of the staff provides the advantage of being able to attack the saber user before he gets into attack range. From another view the selection to deliver a strike could telegraph the swordsman and provide time to close the distance and use the shorter weapon to his advantage. I will go into this more in another aspect, so for now practice the distance drill again with your partner armed with a training sword and explore the relationship of distance and time to an opponent armed with a shorter weapon.

Aspect of Position

Changing position or moving outside or inside the box, as depicted in Figure 155, can overcome the advantages of both distance and time. Remember, the circle moves with each individual, and when you deal with position you are attempting to position yourself at an angle to give you an advantage.

Depending on the length of your weapon, it may be smarter to operate inside instead of outside.

In some circumstances you can change position and range simultaneously and create openings. Face off with your training partner in a middle guard, as you did earlier. Practice moving off your partner's line A and take a half step forward and to your right. Your partner should remain stationary to allow you to see the openings that this movement created at high-, mid-, and low-line levels. Repeat this exercise until you are comfortable with the method and then switch roles with your partner to allow him to experiment with the technique. Throughout this exercise remember that this imaginary circle moves with you as an aid to estimating range and determining position. When it's all said and done, it is a means of imprinting a concept that will eventually become second nature.

Now let's take a closer look at how individual circles relate to the concept of inside and outside the box. In Figure 156 I've included the figures depicting the two aspects of the concept of inside and outside the box. Figure 156C is the more traditional/historical approach based on the sword, which

Aspects of Position

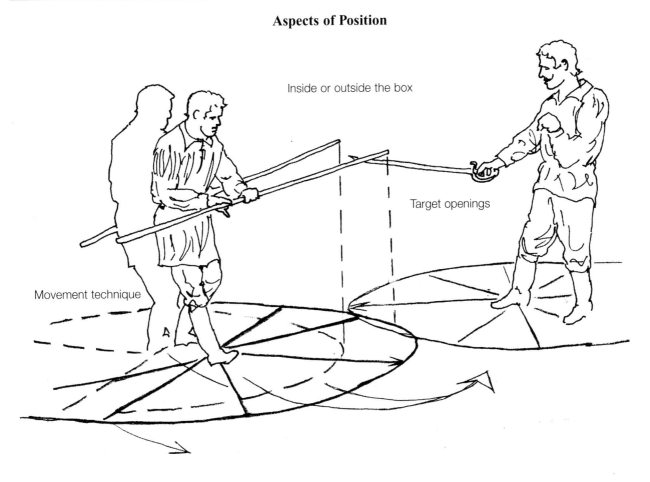

FIGURE 155

requires familiarity when working against an opponent armed with similar weapons. You use this when changing hand and staff positions where foot movements are not very expansive. Figures 156A and B represent my take on an Asian approach that seems to work when the opponent is equipped with shorter or multiple weapons. Foot and body movements to get to the outside tend to be very expansive with long steps. Let's take a quick look at how this positioning works.

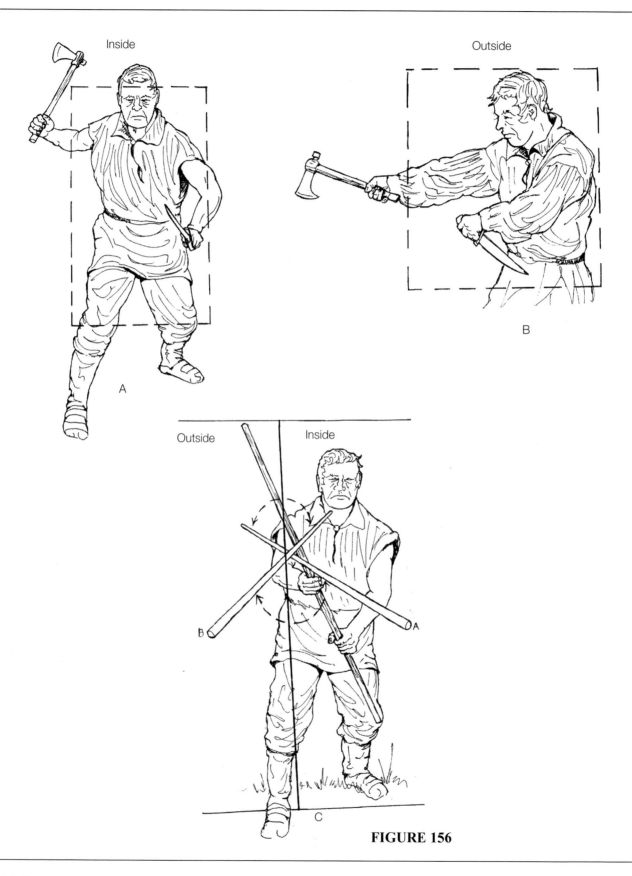

Inside

Outside

A

B

Outside   Inside

B

A

C

FIGURE 156

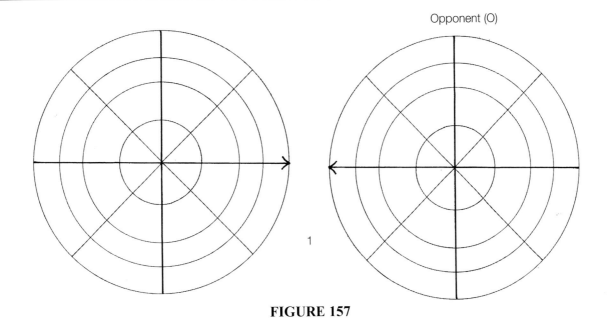

Opponent (O)

1

FIGURE 157

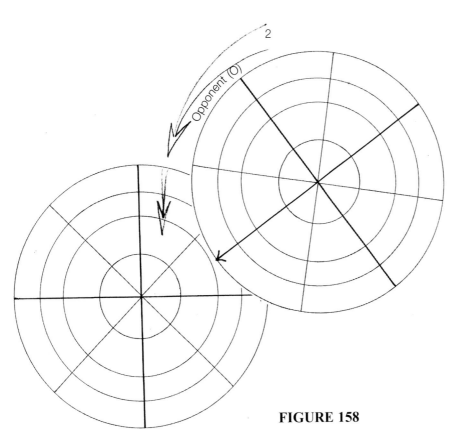

2

Opponent (O)

In Figure 157 your opponent faces you just out attack range. For example, let's say that he is armed with a staff, as depicted in Figure 156C. You both are equally matched in terms of range and can attack both inside and outside with equal ease. In Figure 158 the opponent makes a movement to his left and then abruptly changes direction to his right while moving his circle forward. Simultaneously, he executes an Angle 1 attack to the left side of your head. To counter this you withdraw backward, moving your circle out of range and then step to the opponent's left as visualized in Figure 159. This action gives you the target opportunities illustrated in Figure 160.

FIGURE 158

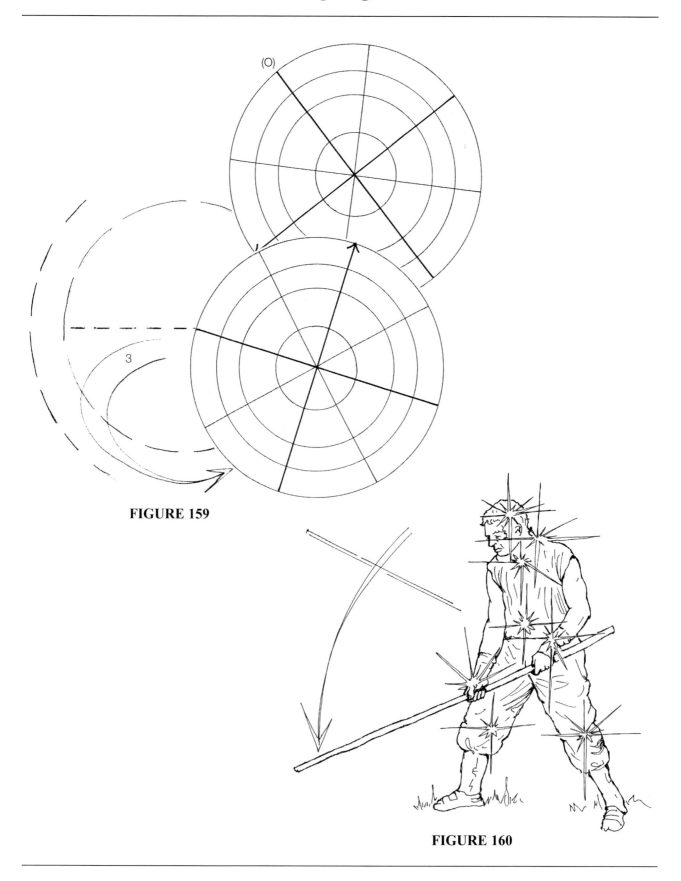

FIGURE 159

FIGURE 160

So there is the concept in a nutshell. I know that I keep saying this, but remember that this circle business is a conceptual training aid used to teach the concept of range and position.

"Combat is the disposition of various blows . . ."
—Unknown author, *Manuscript I.33*

READ THE MESSAGE OF THE OPPONENT, WEAPON, ENVIRONMENT, AND MIND

Whenever you face a potential opponent, there are some conceptual factors that affect the aspects of distance, time, and position just addressed. Basically, these are the messages of the opponent, the weapon, and the environment, which all combine to form a situational awareness that can be used to your advantage. In addition to the circle, they also help provide scope and direction to your training curriculum for the staff.

The *message of the opponent* is concerned with the opponent's body type, attitude, and potential fighting style and the effect they may have on your strategy. The *message of the weapon* carried by the opponent is compared to yours in terms of any advantage he has in range, as well as the techniques to be used by both parties. "How long is his weapon?" "Must I close with him to gain advantage, or will I have to use my advantage of range to overcome him?" "Does he have two weapons?" "Will our weapons dictate closing the distance or fight at range?" These are some of the questions you must ask yourself. The *message of the environment* is another critical point in terms of being able to counter an opponent's advantage or capitalize on your own. Visibility, soil or floor conditions, the amount of usable space must all be considered. The final consideration is the *message of the mind*. "Am I pressed for time?" "Am I afraid or confident?" "How does my skill level compare with that of my opponent, or will I have to use deceit and trickery to overcome him?"

With all this said, I think what is needed is a real-world historical example of how these messages apply. As I explore this, please understand that this attempt to get inside the mind of an individual fighting for his life is pure conjecture on my part. I have to admit exercising a little artistic license for the sake of presenting the messages of the opponent, weapon, environment, and mind in a plausible manner as the combatant *might have done*. I've researched the writings of the individuals in this example and can only give my take on the dynamics of the fight.

"And my pretent being confideth altogether upon the soldier (blunt, plaine, and unpolished) so must my writings be proceeding from fingers fitted for the pike than the pen."
—Richard Peeke, ca. 1625/26

Duel at Xeres
(Staff vs. Rapier, 15 November 1625)

The Situation
On 22 October 1625 the fleet of the Earl of Essex attacked the Spanish coastal fort of Puntal. After the surrender of the garrison, the English force pushed inland toward the town of Cadiz, encountering little resistance. At some point near the bridge of Suazzo, the troops begin pillaging some well-provisioned wine cellars. Needless to say, the soldiers indulged themselves to excess, and before long a general mutiny broke out, with the troops refusing to advance further. The commander of the land force became frightened and ordered the expedition to return to the ships, with the promise of searching for a rich Spanish merchant fleet from the West Indies.

Part of this expedition was the king's ship *Convertine,* captained by Thomas Porter. Serving as a sailor/soldier on this vessel was Richard Peeke, who, after the land force had departed for Cadiz, went ashore on his own to do some foraging. He soon met up with some of his shipmates returning with oranges and lemons. Tempted by the promise of fresh fruit, Peeke ventured further inland, where he encountered three dead and one wounded Englishmen. While attempting to minister to the wounded man, Peeke was attacked by a mounted Spanish officer (knight) who attempted to trample him. Peeke struck the horseman with his cloak and then pulled him out of the saddle. Drawing his sword, Peeke forced the Spaniard to his knees, from which the latter begged for his life. Like any common man of the time, Peeke proceeded to shake down his captive for money and jewels. Just as he was about to take the Spaniard's horse and return to the ship, 14 Spanish musketeers arrived and surrounded the pair. Peeke used his captive as a shield while he assessed the situation. Obviously a practical man who knew when to take the better part of valor, Peeke promptly surrendered.

As Peeke was being bound, the Spanish knight drew his rapier and slashed the Englishman across the face. His former captive would have run Peeke through, but the musketeers intervened and separated the two. As the Englishman was being escorted through the streets of Cadiz, another soldier from the crowd broke through the escort and stabbed Peeke in the back with a halberd. Peeke stayed in prison in Cadiz for about 18 days, where a local Spanish surgeon treated his wounds. On November 13 Peeke was taken to Xeres for trial before what he called a "Council of War." On November 15, he was brought before the council that consisted of three dukes, four counts, four marquises, and an assortment of nobles and soldiers.

From Peeke's account of the questions he was asked, it is clear that the real intent of this council was that of intelligence gathering, to measure the quality of the English soldiers they would shortly be encountering in the invasion planned for England. During the interrogation, the question of how Peeke was wounded came up. On discovery that the Englishman had spared the life of the same knight who later wounded Peeke when his hands were bound, the Duke of Medina rebuked the Spaniard for his base behavior.

Throughout the council there had been much name-calling from the attending audience, referring to the Englishman as a "henne" (hen). When the council finished laughing at the remark, one of the dukes pointed to the Spanish soldiers in attendance in the hall and inquired whether Peeke thought the English on the invasion would view them as "hennes" next year. Responding to the obvious attempt at humor by the noble, Peeke replied that he thought they would be viewed as "pullets or chick-

ens." On that the Spanish noble asked whether Peeke would like to "fight one of these Spanish pullets." With nothing to lose and facing death by execution, Peeke readily accepted the challenge.

The Englishman's shackles were removed, and he was given a rapier and poniard. Peeke's opponent, Tiago, was a skilled rapier and dagger man, and the two spent considerable time moving into position and exchanging attacks. When Peeke caught Tiago's blade with the guard of the poniard, he immediately closed and swept his opponent's feet, sending him to the floor. Pinning the Spaniard to the floor, Peeke secured his opponent's poniard, stood up, walked over to the duke, and presented the weapons to him.

While impressed with the Englishman's skill, the council was not going to let him off that easily and invited him to fight another opponent. Peeke knew that the council was going to keep providing opponents until sooner or later he would meet his better with the rapier and poniard. The odds were just not there. Sensing this, Peeke stated that he'd be happy to fight again if allowed to use the weapon of his country, the quarterstaff. Shortly after his next opponent appeared, Peeke decided to gamble on the honor of the council members and attempt to impress them with a feat of arms. He addressed the council, stating: "I had a sure friend in my hand, that never failed me, and therefore made little account of that one to play with, and should shew them no sport."

On hearing this, the council asked how many men Peeke desired to fight, to which he replied: "I told them any number under sixe." Amused by the audacity of the Englishman, the council provided two additional opponents, setting the stage for one of the most profound historical examples of the skill and efficiency of the common Englishman armed with a quarterstaff.

The Message of the Opponent
While he waited for a staff to be provided, Peeke studied his three opponents. He noted the elegance of their dress but did not sense the haughty superiority he had often associated with the nobility. His opponents were of average height, and their faces reflected steady resolve. He noted no nervous movement as the Spanish manipulated their weapons,

only smooth, confident moves. There was little doubt in Peeke's mind that these men, who enjoyed prominent social status, had arrived there by their proficiency with arms. These were indeed professional fighting men who had risen through the ranks. They knew their trade and knew how to wait for an opening. They were equally skilled with sword and buckler and rapier and dagger, and perhaps had spent time in the pike formation. Peeke estimated that all three could not only duel with grace and style but brawl with the best of them.

The Englishman anticipated that the initial strategy used against him would be similar to that used on the battlefield: his opponents would advance toward him side by side, not unlike the formation movement of infantry from that time. As they got within range, one would attempt to circle behind him while the others kept him engaged. One would attack to engage him while the others thrust from a different position. The Spanish method of fencing relied on the use of circular movement, with a normal walking pace used to attack and withdraw. There would be none of the deep lunges associated with other European systems. While Peeke doubted his opponents would be familiar with the Continental dueling approach, he did expect them to keep their feet underneath them, with each attack being well grounded and balanced. Peeke was aware that these men had seen him very quickly defeat their comrade using the rapier and dagger. In all probability, they would not be as familiar with the advantages and disadvantages of the staff, and this unknown element might just give him the openings he would need.

The Message of the Weapon

Since there was no true quarterstaff available in the hall, one of the soldiers removed the head from a halberd and handed it to Peeke. The weapon was about 7 feet in length, with a short iron spike attached to the heel of the pole. Though the balance was not exactly what Peeke was accustomed to, it fit his hand well and was made of a good, strong hardwood, which was smooth from repeated use. He would hold the staff in the middle-guard position he had been taught since childhood, with the right leg and hand forward. His left hand would grip the staff

at a point approximately 15 inches from the heel of the staff, not unlike the way described in the earlier works of George Silver. This would not only give him the advantage of range, but also provide sufficient length for him to use the heel of the weapon and the spike.

The Englishman's opponents were equipped with cup-hilt rapiers that were slightly shorter than the type favored in other countries. These were reasonably wide-bladed weapons not too far removed from the standard sword. The weapons clearly had a battlefield application with both cut and thrust capability. The daggers of all three were standard for the time. The blades ran about 12–13 inches in length, and a brass pommel topped each hilt. The cross guard was rather large, with the ends sloped toward the point at an acute angle. Often identified as the poniard, this type of edged weapon was primarily used in the left hand to provide defense in the form of blocks or parries. Peeke clearly recalled that his earlier opponent had made no attempt to attack with the poniard, seemingly content to keep it ready for close-in protection.

The Message of the Environment

The floor of the hall where the fight was to take place was made of large stones tightly fitted together to form a reasonably level surface. Here and there a corner of one of the stones protruded, providing an obvious tripping hazard. Peeke noted these as areas to be avoided and perhaps to be used to his advantage. The interior of the building was wide with plenty of overhead clearance, but the audience—confined by a ring of soldiers—occupied a considerable portion of the space, leaving only a space of about 20 by 15 feet in which to maneuver. The condition of the floor was dry with remarkably good footing. Peeke's shoes were well broken in from constant use on the often-slippery deck of ships. He shifted his feet and found that he could feel the texture of the stones through his thin, well-worn soles. He noted that his opponents' footwear, in contrast, appeared relatively new and had rigid soles, which could very easily affect their movement on the stone surface.

The hall relied on the windows for lighting, which provided a rather dim cast to everything within. Peeke noted that his opponents' weapons were oiled and highly reflective, while the deep brown color of his staff tended to blend with the shadows cast in the interior. It was possible, if he were quick enough, that his opponents might not see an incoming attack from his dark weapon.

The Message of the Mind

As his opponents positioned themselves, Peeke began to evaluate his own situation. The odds were definitely not in his favor, no matter how skilled he was with the staff. As the audience began to cheer his opponents, Peeke resigned himself to the fact that he probably would not come out of this engagement alive. The bottom line was that he had nothing to lose by going all out. If he somehow survived, he would probably be executed anyway, so he determined to give it his best and try to end the engagement as quickly as possible. Peeke had been on his feet for a considerable time, and his wounds now began to stiffen and cause him pain. The potential of the staff to thrust and quickly reign multiple blows from the left and right was to his advantage in trying to end the fight sooner rather than later. He would have to keep his distance to some degree in order to stay out of range of the poniards, but based on his previous engagement, he figured his opponents would rely primarily on the rapier.

Strategy and Application to the Fight

At the signal, all three opponents advanced on Peeke, as he anticipated. He would have preferred to position himself where his opponents were almost in line and he could fight only one at a time, but it was not to be. Just as they came in range, one broke slightly to Peeke's right, attempting to circle behind him. Peeke engaged this threat first by turning toward him and parrying the incoming thrust off line with the tip. As the opponent attempted to recover, Peeke closed in, swinging the butt of the staff around and striking the Spaniard in the head. Almost immediately, Peeke pulled the butt back and drove the iron spike into the throat of this opponent.

Then Peeke stepped around his fallen foe and turned to face the other two. Barely avoiding thrusts from both attackers, Peeke delivered a powerful short strike to the nearer opponent's hand. Hearing a loud crunch as the guard on the rapier bent, Peeke followed up with another blow to the elbow of the attacker's same arm, which sent the rapier spinning across the floor. This opponent dropped his poniard and fell to his knees, holding his damaged elbow.

The last standing opponent attempted another thrust, which Peeke parried to the right and, using the middle of his staff, he drove a violent two-handed blow into the chin of the Spaniard. Without hesitation, Peeke slammed into his opponent's chest, sending him tumbling across the room and into the line of soldiers.

Peeke turned again on his heels, but there was no other movement toward him. One Spaniard was dead on the floor with blood flowing from the throat injury, the second was now prone on the floor holding his arm and moaning. The third was lying among the crowd and making no attempt to move.

Needless to say the Spanish council was very impressed with Peeke's performance. The head of the council, the Duke of Medyna, announced that Peeke was not to be harmed and that he would be set free. One of the nobles embraced Peeke and gave him the cloak off his back. Others gave him money. Ultimately Peeke was escorted to Madrid, where he was presented to the King and Queen of Spain, who offered him a position in their service. Peeke politely declined and returned to England, where he wrote an account of his adventures.

A Reminder: As I mentioned earlier, my description of this fight is for all practical purposes conjecture. I based it on what I could derive from Peeke's personal account and later accounts of his adventure. You might say it falls into the category of "what might have happened" and is presented only to provide a plausible example of how the conceptual messages of the opponent, weapon, and environment work hand in hand with that of distance, time, and position. That's all. Besides, wouldn't this make one hell of a movie?

Well . . . enough of the conceptual adventure stuff! Let's get back to training with the staff.

NOTE: Another point that ties into the concept of using the entire staff is a method for increasing power and leverage when delivering a strike. In the

FIGURE 161

earlier descriptions of the strike, the hands remained basically fixed in position once the strike began. The power of the strike varied, depending on the angle and direction of attack. To overcome this limitation, let's turn to a technique that probably originated in either China or Japan.

Here is what is involved: the strike is delivered in the same manner as described earlier, except the hands are shifted forward or backward during the attack. Here is how it works: when striking with the first quarter of the staff, the lead hand slides back toward the rear hand as the staff begins its descent.

Figure 161 depicts this action. When striking with the first quarter of the staff, as you might with a one-two combination, first extend the lead hand. Next, as the heel is pushed up and over into the strike, the trail hand slides forward, which extends the length of the staff into the strike and increases the momentum. This action is depicted in Figure 162. You should practice this technique using the sequence used in Training Objective 4. Again, after mastering this in the air, switch to a target as you did in Training Objective 5.

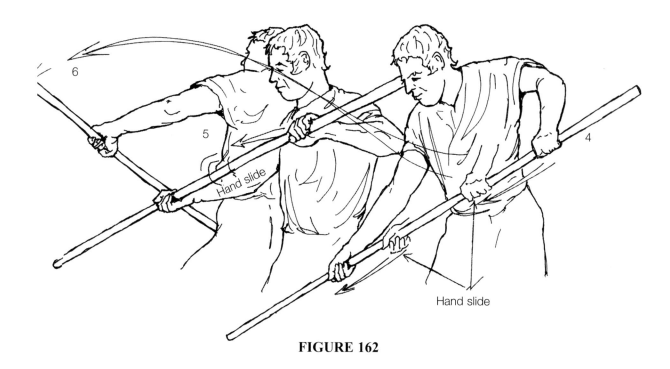

FIGURE 162

NOTE: Earlier we mentioned the use of the swinging bag as a method for determining distance, time, and position. Basically, what this does it teaches you to react to a moving opponent. Because the bag tends to swing at a faster rate than an average person moves, this hones footwork and movement techniques to a much higher standard and consequently is good preparation for full-speed sparring with the staff.

Suspend the swinging bag from a nylon rope in the center of the area in which you will be training. This can be from a rafter or even outside from a rope strung between two trees. Attach a swivel to the bag to permit it to spin when struck. If the structure you are using is strong enough to support it, you may want to use a heavy bag. If not, a lighter bag can be used. I've gotten good results using a 3-inch-diameter bamboo pole. Exercise balls can also work when rigged with a harness. Depending on its length, the bag should be high enough off the ground to hit a person of average height in the chest. There should be enough rope to permit it to swing around in a circle with a diameter of at least 10 feet. So that said, let's begin to look a training objective for the swinging-bag drill.

TRAINING OBJECTIVE 20

Task: Utilize a swinging bag to reinforce the principles of distance, time, and position.

Condition: Given a staff and training area equipped with a swinging bag that swings within a circular area having at least a 10 foot diameter. The drill will begin without weapons where the focus is primarily on getting used to moving around the bag; later weapons will be added and strikes/thrusts delivered to the bag. You may need a training partner to assist in starting and maintaining the speed of the moving bag.

Standard:

Movement Drill 1

Action 1: Assume a middle-guard position without a weapon in front of the bag. Have your training partner pull the back approximately 10 feet in line with your position. On the ready command, your partner should release the bag with a slight push, sending it directly at you.

Action 2: As the bag swings near, pass

Swinging Bag Movement, Drill 1

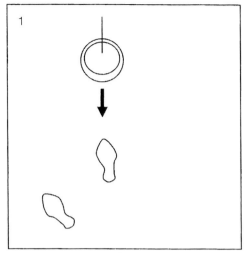
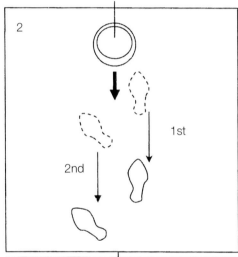
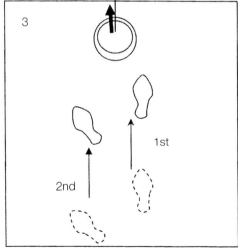

FIGURE 163

the forward leg back past your left. As your right leg stops, immediately pass the left leg back past the right into the original guard position. This movement should take you just out of the maximum extent of the bag's swing and keep it from hitting you.

Action 3: When the bag reaches the limit of its swing and starts to go back in the opposite direction, execute a passing step where the left leg goes forward and past the right. As the left foot lands, execute a pass with the right leg into the original position.

Action 4: As your training partner assists in maintaining the speed of the bag, continue with Actions 2 and 3 until you become proficient in changing and maintaining distance from the moving bag. You probably should repeat this about 10 to 15 times each training session. Figure 163 depicts these actions from an overhead view.

NOTE: In this drill I only illustrated it for the pass forward/pass backward footwork pattern. You will also want to experiment extensively with the other patterns discussed earlier, paying close attention to where the various methods place you in relation to the bag. You will find some more efficient in getting out of the way than others.

Action 5: Once you have mastered the movement with the bag, arm yourself with the staff and practice striking and thrusting the bag as it comes in and moves away.

Movement Drill 2
This drill will focus on the angle left/right aspect of footwork.

Action 1: Assume a middle-guard position without a weapon in front of the bag. Have your training partner pull the back approximately 10 feet in line with your position. On the ready command, your partner should release the bag with a slight

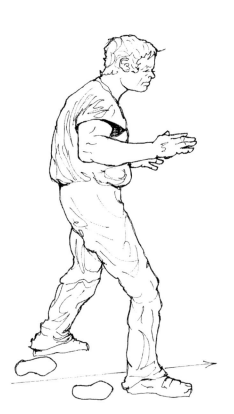

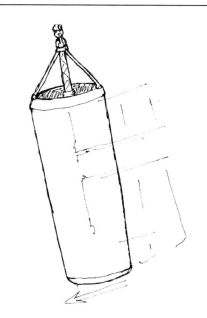

FIGURE 164

push, sending it directly at you.

Action 2: As the bag swings near, execute an angle left foot movement by swinging the left leg around to the right rear as illustrated in Figures 164 and 165.

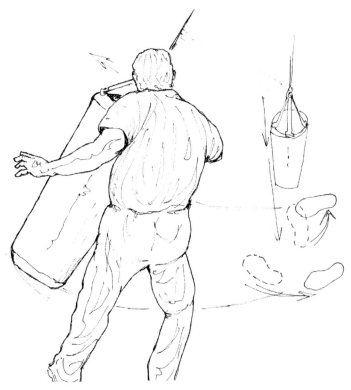

FIGURE 165

FIGURE 166

Action 3: When the bag swings back move into the original middle-guard position, as depicted in Figure 166.

FIGURE 167

Action 4: As the bag comes back toward you a second time, avoid it by executing an angle right foot movement. This time the right leg should swing around to the left rear, as demonstrated in Figure 167.

NOTE: Figures 168 and 169 depict the footwork in Actions 1–4.

Swinging Bag Movement, Drill 2

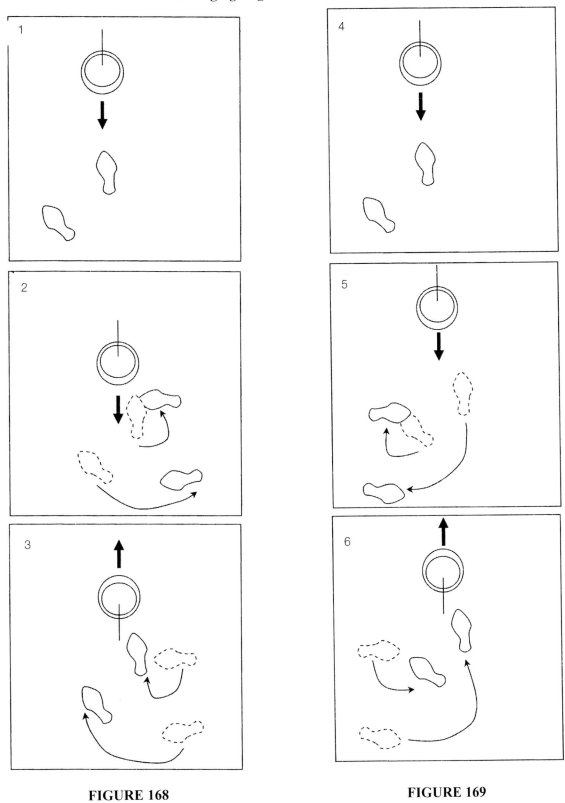

FIGURE 168   FIGURE 169

FIGURE 170

Action 5: Arm yourself with a staff and execute the footwork patterns against the bag while striking and thrusting. Figures 170 through 173 depict this sequence.

NOTE: As with Movement Drill 1, you will also want to experiment extensively with the other patterns discussed earlier, paying close attention to where the various methods place you in relation to the bag. You will find some more efficient in getting out of the way than others.

Movement Drill 3

This free-flowing drill sharpens the movement and attack skills by inducing unpredictable direction changes into the swinging bag. You begin by taking up a position in the center of the circle. Your training partner pulls the bag to its extreme limit on the outer circumference of the circle. On command, he forcefully pushes the bag in the direction of the circle. You adjust your position by moving forward to intercept the bag as it spirals in to the center. Using either a striking or thrusting technique, you attack the bag, which will normally change the direction of the bag. Your training partner will move rapidly to the bag and send it immediately back at you in either a straight line or spiral. Using your footwork-movement patterns, avoid the bag and move to a position to attack it when it comes back around. Throughout this drill, alternate between avoiding and attacking. Be careful not to knock the hell out of your training partner when he moves

FIGURE 171

in to push the bag. This drill is a good transition into and out of range sparring, which I will discuss later.

FIGURE 172

FIGURE 173

CHAPTER 14
ASPECTS OF PARTNER DRILL

Now is a good time to expand a bit on the striking and thrusting capability explored earlier. You'll do this with a series of drills with a training partner. These exercises are designed to improve hand-eye coordination and reinforce muscle memory in the execution of offensive and defensive techniques. These drills should never become an end in themselves.

Drills are just a small part of a training regimen geared toward making you a better fighter, not a drill expert or forms competitor. Today there are groups of well-meaning, incredibly fit martial artists whose weapons practice looks more like gymnastics. It is easy to get caught up in the choreography of a well-executed, acrobatic two-man set. While I really enjoy watching these exhibitions of beauty and skill, I view them as being closer to entertainment or sport rather than an application to actual fighting. Don't get me wrong: these programs are characterized by an intense practice regimen and awesome conditioning program, but the focus is more on being visually impressive than on being applicable to real combat. There is a place for this type of training in the martial arts, and there are things to be learned from their practice. Just keep in mind that drills or two-man sets are but gears in the complex machine of preparing for action.

BASIC RULES FOR PARTNER TRAINING

Point 1: Partner training is *not* competition between you and your training partner. It is also *not* an opportunity to exercise your ego through the superiority of your martial skills. Every one has run across people like this. They usually attempt to counter the technique you are practicing rather than functioning as a training aid for you. The bottom line is that a training partner should always stay within the context of the technique/drill being practiced and do his job as a training aid.

Point 2: Partner training is *not* an opportunity to socialize. Keep all conversation direct and oriented to the drill/technique at hand. Make sure that both partners understand the signals for when to begin and end the drill.

Point 3: Begin all drills slowly and increase the speed based on mutual agreement of both partners.

Point 4: Remember that the focus of drills is primarily to familiarize you with the weapon and improve your reaction time. Standard drills often include movements that require you to return to a neutral position instead of following through with an additional attack. Don't let this bother you; you will work through this aspect later when practicing the engagement scenarios.

DRILL SETS

To conserve space, I've only included three drill sets that address the fundamental staff techniques. You will find many more of these in the various Asian and Western disciplines today. I encourage readers to search the various Internet sources for additional drills to enhance their training regimens. One of my favorites is that of the British Quarterstaff Association located at http://www.quarterstaff.org/. Go to its gallery section and click on the online drill videos. Below are the training objectives for your drill sets.

TRAINING OBJECTIVE 21

Task: Execute Drill Sets 1, 2, and 3 with a training partner.

Condition: You need a staff and a training area sufficient to accommodate 360-degree movement

and overhead strikes with the staff. The focus of these drills is to improve your proficiency in striking and thrusting with the staff against a defending training partner.

Standard: Each training partner is operating as both attacker and defender for a given set of strikes or thrusts. You should practice these drills progressively from slow to moderate to full speed. Once you are proficient, be sure to switch roles so that you can become familiar with the total variety of attacks and defense. Each drill should be repeated 10–15 times before alternating.

Drill Set 1
In this set you will use two views to assist in visualizing the various techniques. The first will be a side view, like that depicted in Figure 174. For this set, think of yourself as the figure on the right with your training partner/opponent on the left. Figure 175

FIGURE 174

FIGURE 175

presents a view from your position, with the staff "floating" in an approximate position in relation to your training partner as seen.

Action 1: Begin the drill with both part-ners assuming a middle-guard position. As you advance into striking distance of your training partner, he shifts slightly to his left and draws back his staff, as depicted in Figures 174 and 175.

FIGURE 176

Action 2: As soon as his staff is withdrawn, your partner delivers an Angle 8 attack to your head with the fourth quarter of his staff. Immediately you slide forward and execute a high block, as illustrated in Figures 176 and 177.

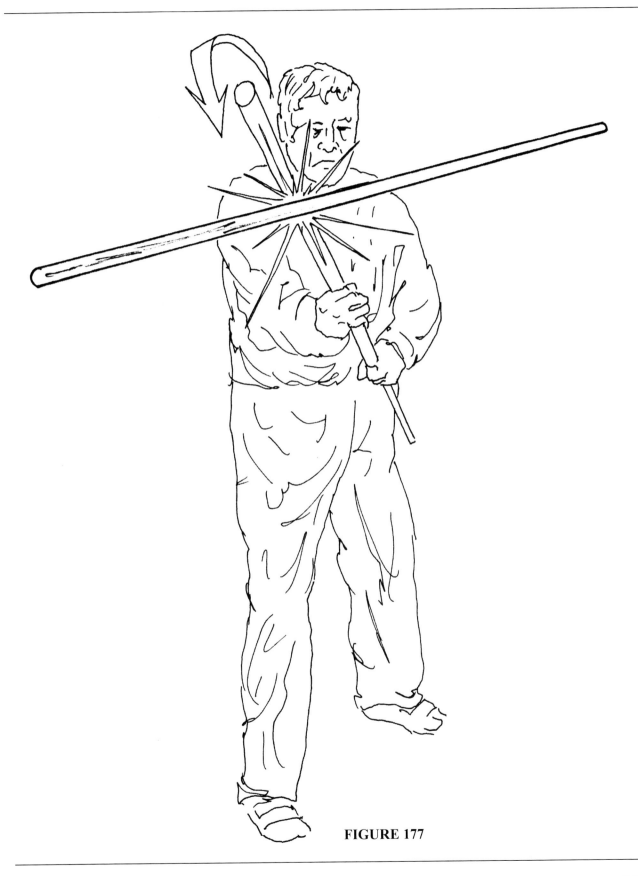

FIGURE 177

FIGURE 178

Action 3: In reaction to your block, your training partner steps forward and executes an Angle 7 attack with the first quarter of the staff to your groin area. You immedi- ately pull your right leg to the rear and execute a low block to the incoming strike. This is illustrated in Figures 178 and 179.

FIGURE 179

FIGURE 180

Action 4: In reaction to your block, your training partner executes an Angle 3 attack to your left side using the first quarter of the staff. Instantly you execute a vertical block to your left, as depicted in Figures 180 and 181.

FIGURE 181

FIGURE 182

Action 5: In response, your training partner executes an Angle 4 attack to your right side using the fourth quarter of the staff. You immediately reply with a vertical block to your right, as depicted in Figures 182 and 183.

FIGURE 183

Action 6: On completion of Action 5, both training partners return to the middle-guard start position. This completes the first drill set. Don't forget to alternate roles with your partner.

• • •

"If you know well the advantages of different weapons, you can use any weapon appropriately in accordance with the situation of the moment. You should not have a predilection for certain weapons. Putting too much emphasis on one weapon results in not having enough of others."
　　　　　　—Miyamoto Musashi, 1643

Figure 184 depicts the aspect that Musashi addressed above in the quote from *Go Rin No Sho.* I've included it as a reminder that it is really important to train using the staff against a variety of weapons. Over the years I have tried to apply this theory to weapons that are entirely different from the one that is the primary focus of the curriculum. Not only does this expose the student to the advantages and disadvantages of a variety of weapons, but it also serves as a starting point for introducing new weapons into the training.

Drill Set 2

For this drill set, I've selected the saber, whose cutting and guard patterns have applications to many of today's weapons. You could just as easily choose a machete, bowie knife, or whatever you. If you are a history buff, you could use a rapier or sword and buckler. It does not matter whether the weapon is historically relevant or applicable to today's modern world. What is important is getting the experience of dealing with a variety of capabilities to expand your knowledge for dealing with the "message of the weapon." Just for the hell of it, I used the broadsword cut-and-guard diagram

FIGURE 184

FIGURE 185

described by Donald Walker in his 1840 text Defensive Exercises. It is a matter of what your training priorities are.

This set utilizes the same two-view illustration approach addressed in Drill Set 1. Your opponent should be equipped with a wooden training saber. To save wear and tear on your staff, I recommend not using blunted steel or aluminum training sabers.

Action 1: Take up a position in range of your training partner. The saber partner should assume a middle-guard position, similar to that depicted in Figure 185, with the right leg forward. The staff partner should begin with the left leg forward, depicted at the left in Figure 185.

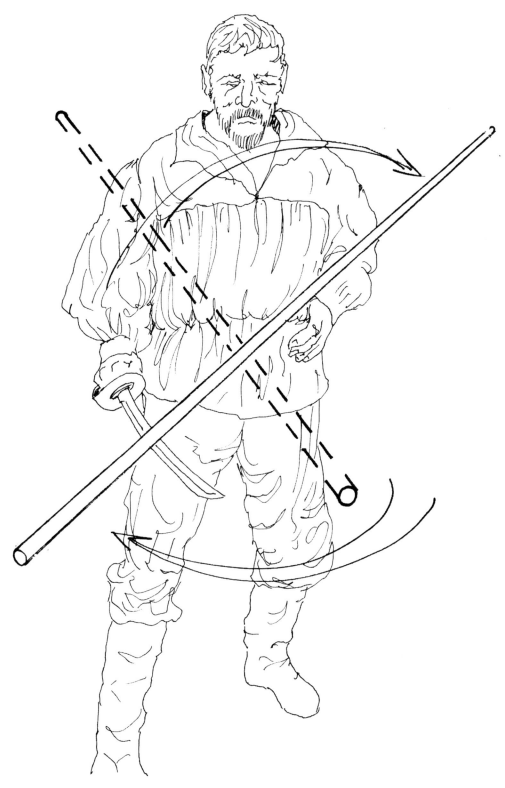

FIGURE 186

FIGURE 187

Action 2: The staff partner begins the drill by changing hands from the left to right side, similar to that depicted in Figure 186. As his staff comes across, he steps forward delivering an Angle 5 strike to the inside of the saber partner's lead leg.

Immediately, the saber partner drops his point and executes a third-guard block to the incoming staff as depicted in Figures 187 and 188. See Figure 189 for Walker's cut-and-guard diagram.

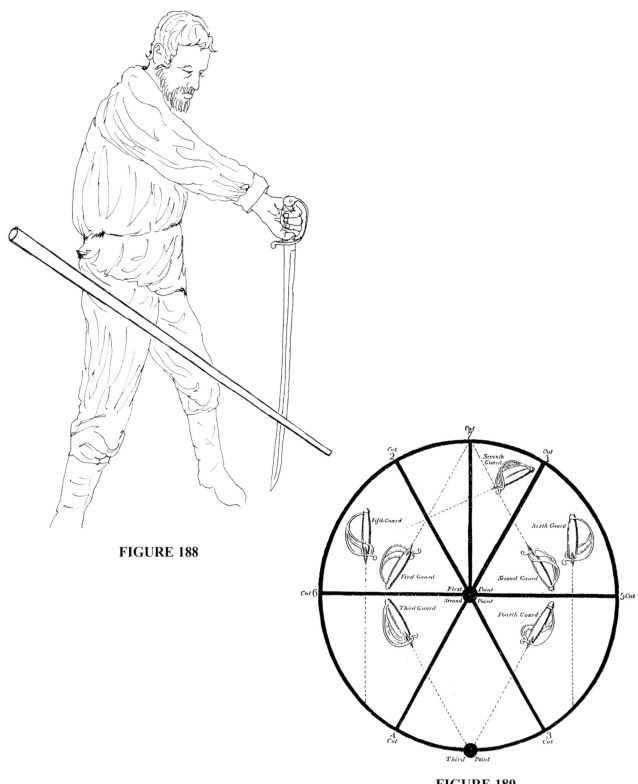

FIGURE 188

FIGURE 189

Donald Walker's cut-and-guard diagram.

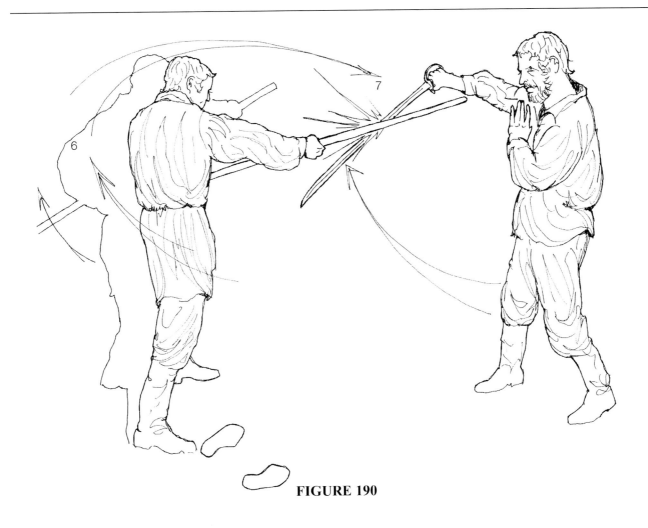

FIGURE 190

Action 3: Immediately on the block, the staff partner retracts his staff and delivers an Angle 1 attack to the saber partner's head.

Simultaneously the saber partner executes a seventh-guard block to the incoming staff strike, as depicted in Figures 190 and 191.

FIGURE 191

FIGURE 192

Action 4: The saber partner slides his weapon off the staff and delivers a Cut 1 (from Walker's diagram, Figure 189) to the staff partner's neck. Immediately, the staff partner swings his right leg around to the rear and delivers an Angle 2 strike to deflect the incoming saber cut, as seen in Figures 192 and 193.

FIGURE 193

FIGURE 194

Action 5: On deflection, the staff partner executes a straight horizontal thrust with the first quarter of the staff at his opponent's head. The saber partner swings his right leg back and to the rear while executing the high-line parry depicted in Figure 194. Both partners move back into middle-guard position. This completes the drill.

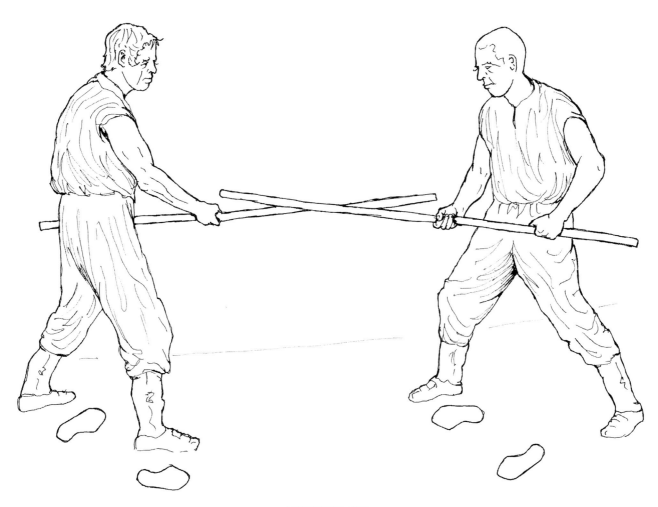

FIGURE 195

Drill Set 3

This set utilizes the same two-view illustrations seen previously. The focus is on countering the high-line thrust and delivering an immediate counterstrike.

NOTE: To accommodate the restrictions of paper size, it was necessary to illustrate the training partners closer than they would normally be.

Action 1: As depicted in Figures 195 and 196, both training partners should approach each other in a middle-guard position. In these drawings, you are the training partner on the left.

FIGURE 196

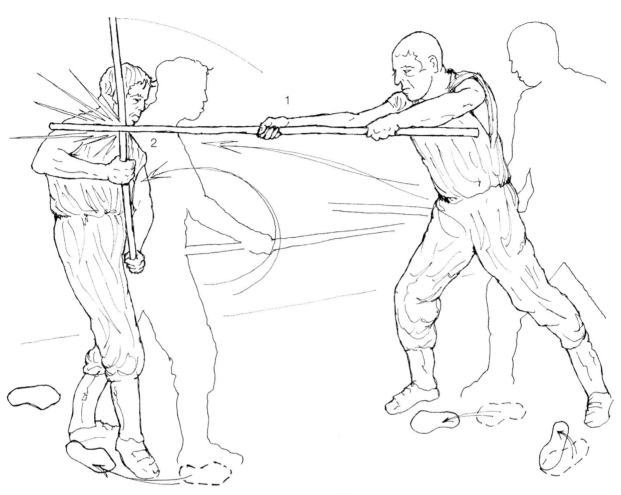

FIGURE 197

Action 2: As your partner gets within range, he opens the set by executing a straight thrust to your neck. You immediately move your staff back and to the left, deflecting its path off to your right.

Simultaneously, you swing your lead leg around to the rear, as depicted in Figure 197. The approximate positions of both partners' weapons appear in Figure 198.

FIGURE 198

FIGURE 199

Action 3: Immediately on the deflection, you roll the fourth quarter of the staff over into an Angle 8 attack to your opponent's head. Your training partner pivots to his left while moving the third quarter of the staff up into a high horizontal guard that deflects the incoming strike, as depicted in Figures 199 and 200.

Action 4: Both you and your training partner return to the middle-guard position and begin the exercise again as needed.

FIGURE 200

CHAPTER 15

ASPECTS OF THE CLOSE-QUARTER FIGHT

"It often happens that both staves makes contact in the middle. When this happens to you, keep your staff on his and let go with your left hand, moving it back, and then make sure you have a grip on both weapons. Move your back end under his and across. Push your staff with your right hand over and in towards yourself. This will force him to let go of his staff or to fall, if you place your right foot behind him."

—Joachim Meyer, 1570

Our German friend is addressing a fight for which circumstances may not permit the weapon to be used to its true potential. He is operating with the staff under less-than-ideal conditions of close-quarter combat. Some weapons are best suited for fighting at long or medium ranges, and while such is the case for the staff, its potential for use at close quarters is also impressive. Remember earlier discussion devoted to determining distance? Figure 151 (page 132) shows an aspect of the Spanish circle depicted as a floor diagram. Figure 201 depicts this same circle, only this time I've indicated the close-quarter ranges in a heavier line. Here, for all practical purposes, your opponent will be in your face, so to speak. In these situations where you are staff-to-staff with your

opponent, a great deal of pushing, pinning, pulling, slipping, and levering goes on to get your weapon into position to strike. When compounded with kicks, posts, and sweeps using the feet and legs, this can be a pretty nasty position to be in. This section addresses this scenario when you are facing an opponent armed with a similar staff-like weapon.

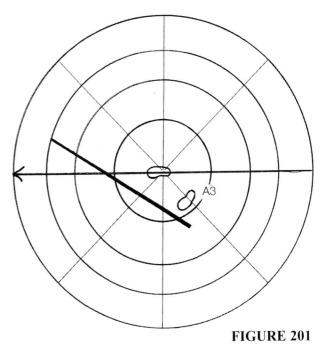

FIGURE 201

Often close-quarter engagements begin when opponents close within the A3 circle depicted in Figure 201. Here the staff may end up initially in the staff-on-staff position illustrated in Figures 202A and B. You can execute a variety of slipping, pinning, pushing, and pulling techniques by moving the staff through a series of horizontal and vertical positions, in an attempt to gain access or openings above the arms, under the arms, or below the waist, and to position yourself in front of and behind your opponent's legs.

The directional arrows in Figures 202A, 202B, and 203 illustrate the motions. These movements involve controlling and reacting to your opponent's staff through a series of side-to-side motions (shown in Figure 203), and a sliding up-and-down movement, as shown in Figure 204. Figure 205 shows how these movements (up and down, left and right, back and forth) are involved with manipulating your staff to get access to target areas above the arms, under the arms, blow the waist, and in front/behind the legs. Figure 206 illustrates these areas as they relate to the first and fourth quarters of the staff. Figure 207 depicts these generic areas, while Figure 208 shows the relationship of the various quarters of the staff to the target areas.

FIGURE 202B

FIGURE 202A

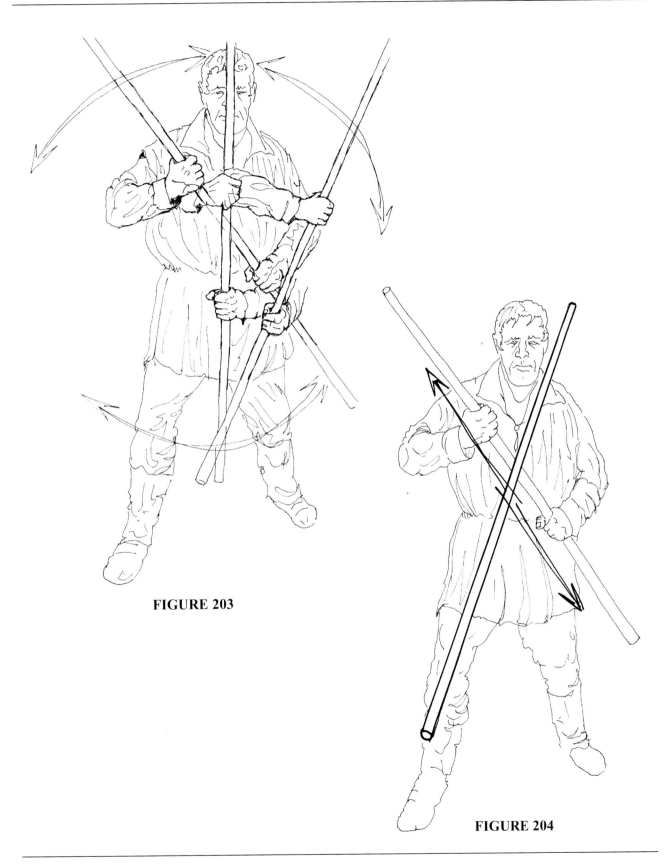

FIGURE 203

FIGURE 204

Above arms

Under arms

Below waist

Front and
behind legs

FIGURE 205

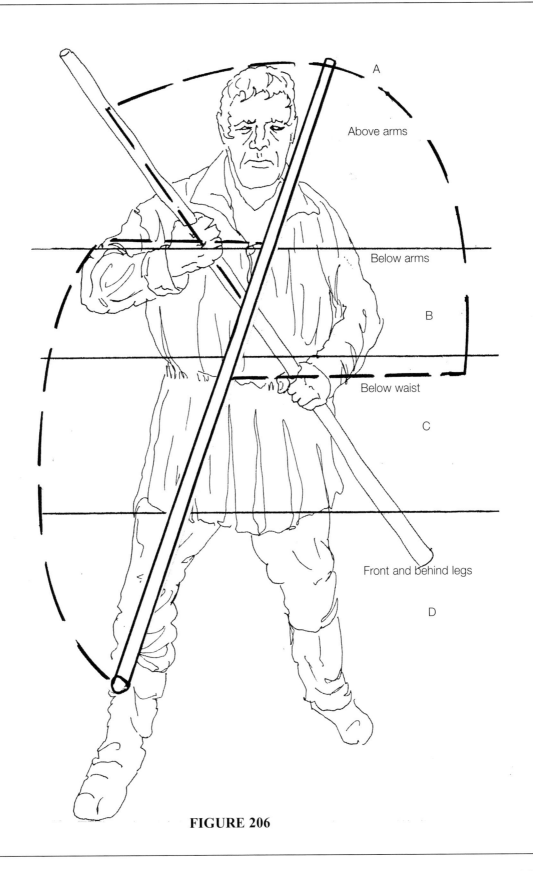

A

Above arms

Below arms

B

Below waist

C

Front and behind legs

D

FIGURE 206

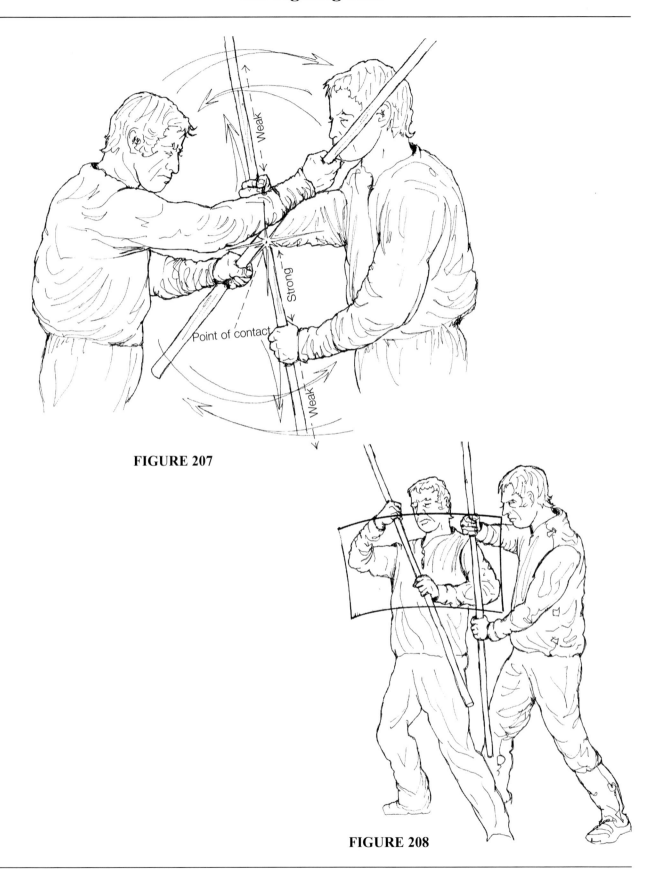

FIGURE 207

FIGURE 208

Let's examine this a bit further in Figure 207. The key to everything discussed up to now is centered on what happens at that point of staff-on-staff contact. Both you and your opponent can maneuver your weapon up and down, left and right, or back and forth, using this point of contact as a fulcrum. From this point you can push, pull, or pin with your staff to strike, thrust, or execute a disarm by levering against an opponent's limbs. In this situation you are feeling your opponent's movement through your staff and reacting to pressure along the strong and weak portions of the staff. Remember that the area between the hands is the strong, stable portion, and it is that part that usually makes contact first when things get close.

PINNING

Pins are normally executed with the strong part of the staff between the hands. In most cases, the opponent's forearm or upper arm is pressed close to his body and in the area indicated in Figure 208. It should also be noted that a pin can be directed against either the strong or weak portion of the opponent's staff, as illustrated earlier in Figure 207. A pin usually follows some form of impact as one of the opponents forcefully jams his weapon into the area. Pins can be used to establish a point of contact from which to pivot under the opponent's arms, similar to that indicated in Figures 209 and 210. Both figures present a situation where a violent, forceful, two-handed strike or push is delivered to the opponent's rib cage.

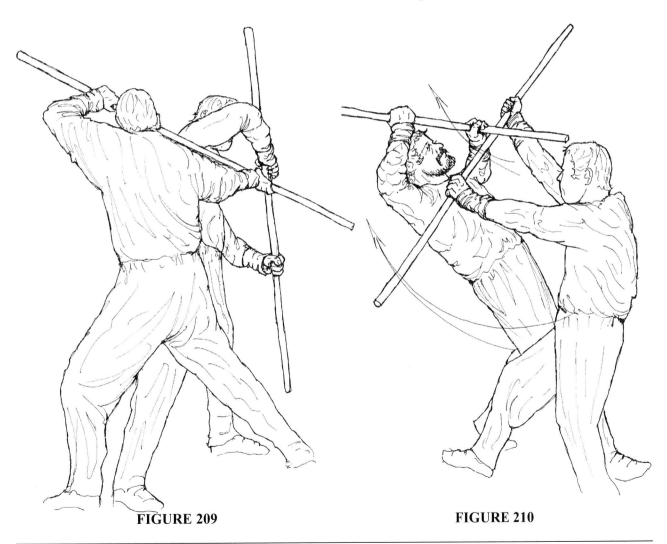

FIGURE 209 **FIGURE 210**

PUSHING

A push usually is preceded by a pin and can be directed against either the strong or weak portion of your opponent's staff or torso. Figure 209 illustrates a push being directed against an opponent's upper rib cage and staff. Figure 210 shows an upward push to drive an opponent's arms and create an opening for a second push against his chest. Just as with the pin, a push can be executed on impact. An interesting technique is to target an opponent's hand during this action (Figure 211). Pushing techniques are useful against joints in such low-line areas as the knees.

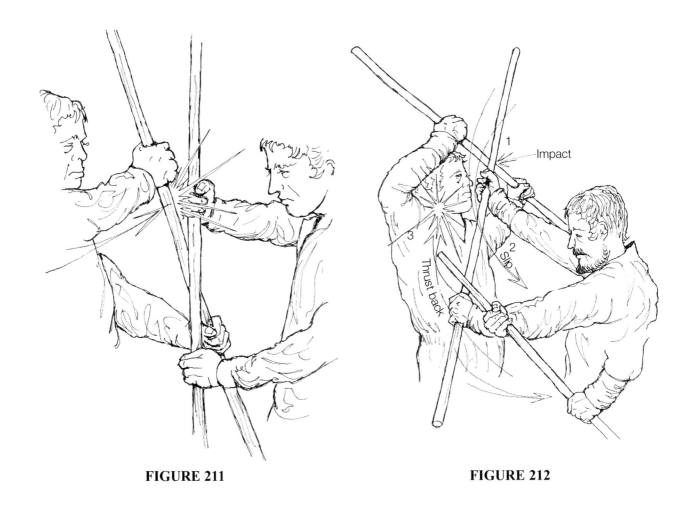

FIGURE 211

FIGURE 212

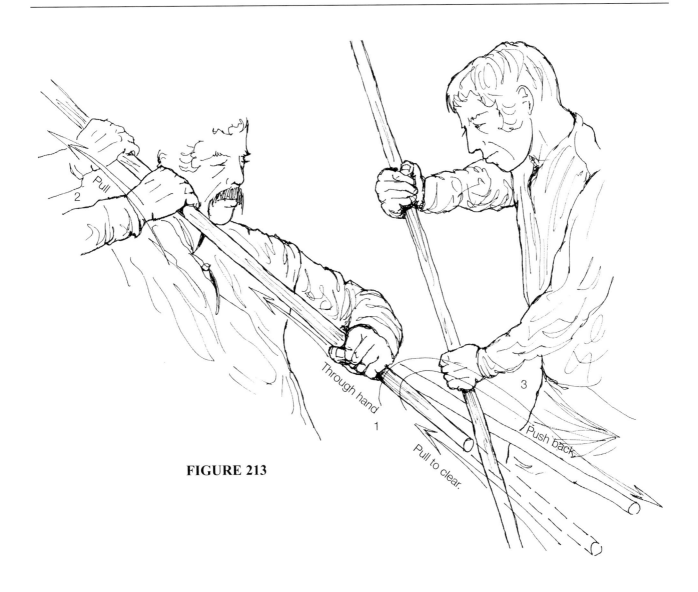

FIGURE 213

SLIPPING

This technique involves making contact with either the first or fourth quarter of the staff and then sliding that quarter off the opponent's weapon and immediately striking or thrusting back along the same line. Figure 212 illustrates the slip, following an opponent's horizontal high-line block. Here you pull the staff forcefully to the rear, to the point where the tip slips off the opponent's staff, and deliver an immediate thrust back along the same line into the opponent's face. Figure 213 illustrates the slip against a low-line block where the staff is moved over the opponent's staff to the inside for a position to lever against his legs or thrust the knees. During close-quarter engagements, there may not be enough room to execute the slip. When this occurs, you can shorten the staff by sliding it through one hand or the other. This is also demonstrated in Figure 213.

FIGURE 214

LEVERING

This technique involves maneuvering your staff between (or over/under) the opponent's arms or staff and then pulling back in the opposite direction against the arms, neck, or torso. Figure 214 illustrates this technique, where the staff is levered against an opponent's arm and neck to topple him backward. These techniques are often used in conjunction with trips, kicks, or sweeps.

Figure 215 demonstrates the lever between an opponent's arms, where a push-pull action twists the opponent's weapon around and over, resulting in a disarm. Levering can also be accomplished by thrusting the staff between an opponent's legs and then moving quickly in the opposite direction, as seen in Figure 216.

FIGURE 215

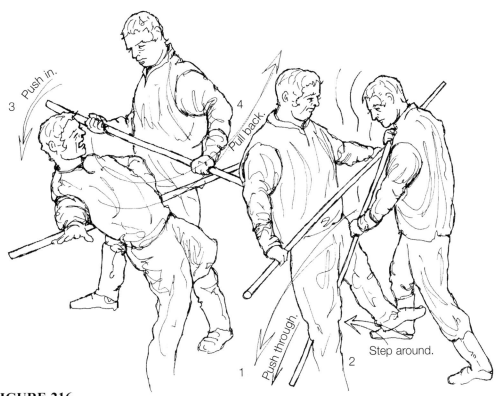

FIGURE 216

PULLING

This aspect can consist of looping the staff behind an opponent's weapon, hand, arm, or legs, and pulling like hell. It can also be as simple as just grabbing with one of your hands. Figures 217 through 220 illustrate some common pulls.

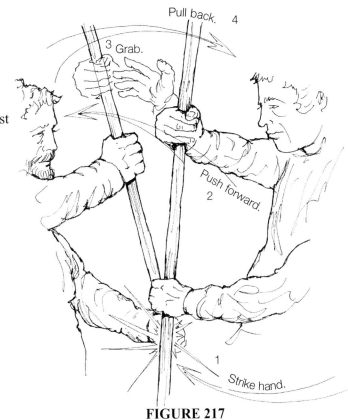

FIGURE 217

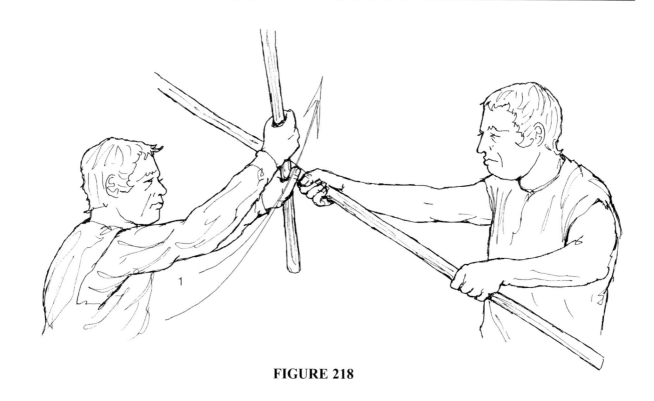

FIGURE 218

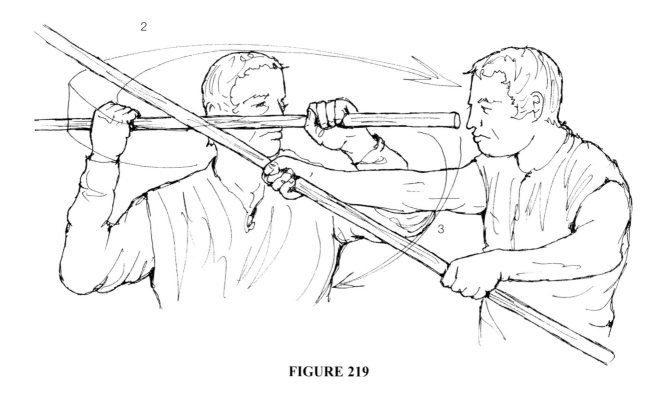

FIGURE 219

FIGURE 220

TRAINING OBJECTIVE 22

Task: Experiment with the various close-quarter staff techniques of pinning, pushing, slipping, levering, and pulling.

Condition: You need a staff and training area sufficient to accommodate 360-degree movement and overhead strikes with the weapon. The focus of this training is to become familiar with the close-quarter techniques with a training partner. You should practice each technique, with each partner assuming the opponent's role. In this role, the partner will provide moderate resistance as you execute the technique to help you master the method. Refer to Figures 202 through 220 for each specific exercise.

Standard: Begin the exercise by taking up a position in the middle guard approximately 5 feet from your training partner.

Action 1: Experiment with pinning and pushing. Using Figures 202A and B (page 182) as a guide, both partners should move to contact with the staffs (similar to that in illustration A). Don't knock the hell out of each other but give a good bump to that strong portion of the staff so that you feel the impact. Practice pushing your partner backward and then letting him push you backward while using both advancing and passing steps. Note the amount of ground that you give up or take with the advancing step. Notice also how easy it is to push your partner back when his feet are in line, as well as how hard it is to push when he has one leg forward. What is the message here? Watch his feet! When he starts to take a step, *push the hell out of him*. Each partner should practice breaking contact with the opponent by executing a violent shove and then stepping back. Note how, when you give ground, openings appear for strikes.

Action 2: Experiment with slipping the staff up and down (left and right) along the opponent's staff. Again, using Figures 202A and Figure 204 as guides, practice sliding your staff up and down in the strong portion of the staff. Note the resistance you get the closer you get to the opponent's hands. Practice jumping your staff over both his upper and lower hands to impact on the weaker portion of the staff toward the tip and heel. While practicing this, note the opening for strikes both to the left and right sides, similar to that depicted in Figure 207 (page 186). Note how the staff can be pivoted left and right for openings, similar to the movement depicted in Figure 203 (page 183).

Action 3: Experiment with slipping and thrusting, using the shortening technique. Take a position in front of your training partner just within range for a long strike. Execute a long strike to your partner's head while he simultaneously executes a high horizontal block, as depicted in Figure 219. On impact, you slide and push your forward hand up against his staff and then immediately begin to pull your staff to the rear. When this action is under way, begin to pull your staff through the lead hand till it slips off the opponent's staff. As the staff clears, immediately execute a thrust upward into the head area.

SAFETY NOTE: Be very careful to perform this technique only in slow motion so that you do not injure your partner. I strongly recommended that you practice this only with a padded staff and adequate throat protection.

You will also want to practice this shortening technique into the low-line areas as well. Begin by executing a low-line strike to your partner's legs. When he blocks it, execute a slip/shortening technique over his staff into a thrust to his knees, similar to that indicated in Figure 213 (page 189).

Action 4: Experiment with the levering techniques. As you did with Actions 1–3, take up a middle-guard position facing your training partner within striking range. Your partner delivers a slow-speed vertical strike to your head. You execute a high-line horizontal block. Immediately on impact, pivot to your left on your opponent's staff and pull back to allow it to clear his head/neck area with the heel of the staff, as indicated in Figure 214 (page 190). As soon as the heel clears, push the staff through the trail hand, extending it in front of your partner's neck, and then forcefully pull back and lever the first quarter of the staff against his neck and arm. If you continue this motion it will ultimately result in your toppling the opponent. This action should also be practiced to the right side. Using Figures 215 through 220 as guides, experiment with the other options for levering and pulling.

NOTE: For safety's sake, make sure you begin the above actions at slow speed and progress to faster action only when both partners have mastered the technique. I recommend that you don adequate head, hand, groin, and elbow protection, along with using a padded staff, before commencing to full-speed practice.

CHAPTER 16
ASPECTS OF KICKING

There are many ideas about the role of kicks when fighting with long weapons, but here I will only address it as a complement to fighting with the close-range techniques just addressed. The advantage of this is simply that low-line kicks delivered from that range do not easily telegraph your intent to your opponent, as do those beautiful, high-line kicks seen in many martial arts. This is not to say there is not a place for those methods; it's just that they should be limited to advanced-level work. For the purposes of teaching the fundamentals, I will discuss four kicks: the straight, inside, sweep, and chain kick.

STRAIGHT KICK

Figures 221 and 222 depict the straight kick initiated with the rear leg immediately following a forward push. This particular kick targets the front of the knee, whereas the heel is driven into the target, locking the joint backward and hyperextending the leg, which usually results in forcing the opponent backward and down. This can be a crippling technique, so when working with a partner, only deliver it at slow speed. Straight kicks can also target an opponent's groin, abdomen, or lower chest (in the last instance, the kick is sometimes referred to as a through-the-heart kick).

FIGURE 221

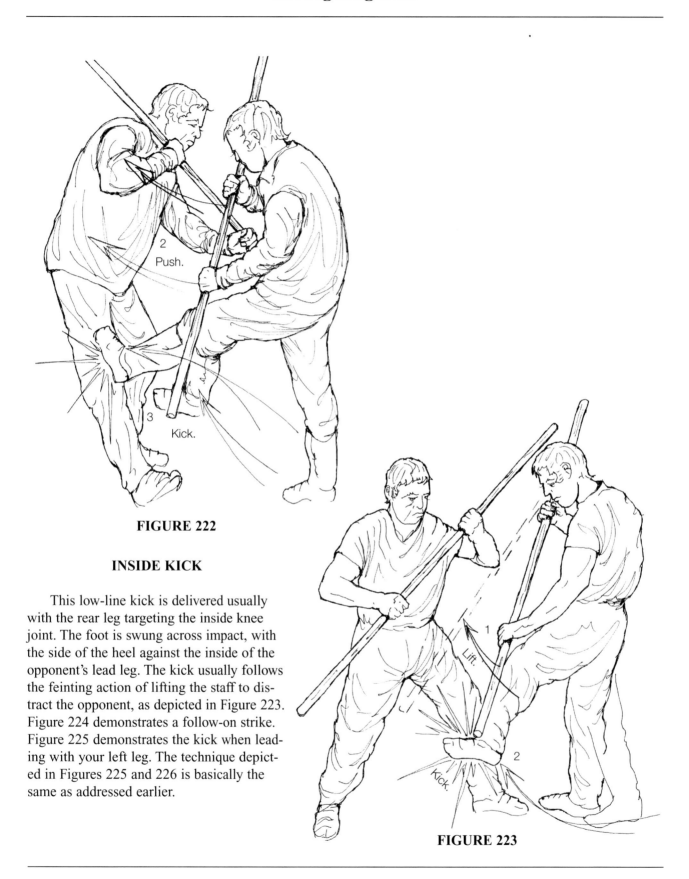

FIGURE 222

INSIDE KICK

This low-line kick is delivered usually with the rear leg targeting the inside knee joint. The foot is swung across impact, with the side of the heel against the inside of the opponent's lead leg. The kick usually follows the feinting action of lifting the staff to distract the opponent, as depicted in Figure 223. Figure 224 demonstrates a follow-on strike. Figure 225 demonstrates the kick when leading with your left leg. The technique depicted in Figures 225 and 226 is basically the same as addressed earlier.

FIGURE 223

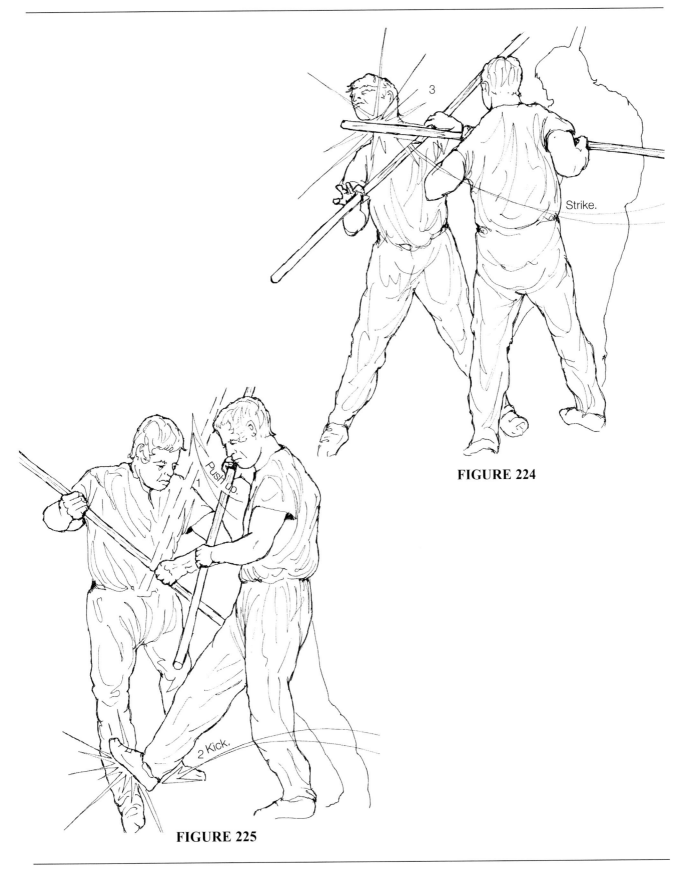

FIGURE 224

FIGURE 225

3 Strike.

FIGURE 226

SWEEP KICK

This technique involves hooking your foot around the ankle of the opponent's lead leg, as depicted in Figure 227. You then complete the action by violently lifting the opponent's leg up and to the

side, which results in the toppling action shown in Figure 228.

As mentioned earlier, there are many more kicking and sweeping aspects that you could learn, but do not attempt those until you have mastered these basics.

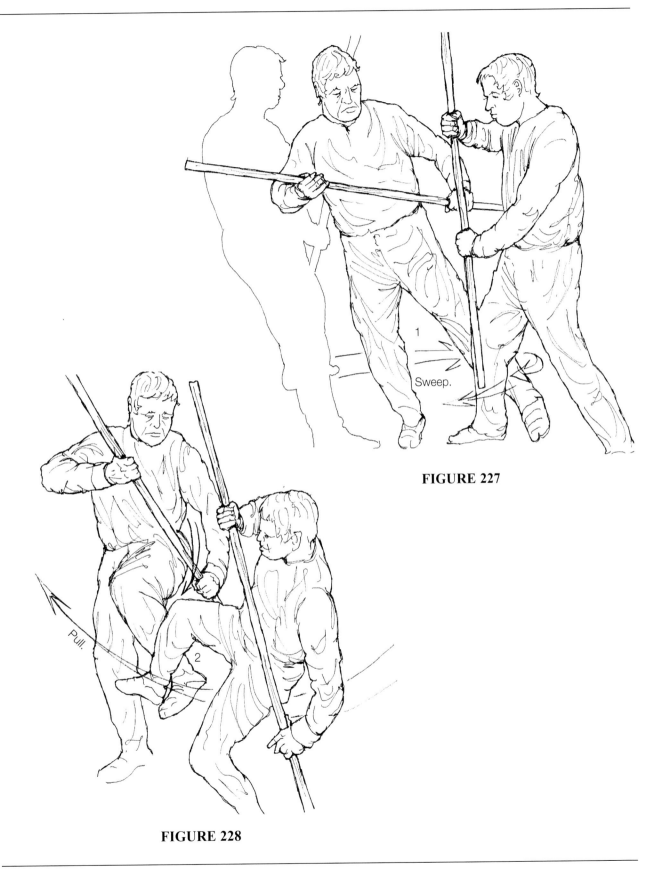

FIGURE 227

FIGURE 228

FIGURE 229

CHAIN KICK

This is a rather common kick in the Asian martial arts. I've chosen to include it here because it is a reasonably low-line kick that seems to work very well in conjunction with a horizontal block.

As shown in Figure 229, the opponent delivers an overhead strike to your head. Immediately after executing a horizontal block, you slide down the opponent's staff and simultaneously leap forward, driving the left leg upward, as depicted in Actions 2

and 3 in Figure 229. As soon as the left leg starts to drop, drive the right knee upward and deliver a kick either to your opponent's hand or midsection as depicted in Figure 230.

TRAINING OBJECTIVE 23

Task: This is the same as Training Objective 22 but with the addition of the kicking and sweeping techniques previously addressed.

FIGURE 230

Condition: You need a staff and training area sufficient to accommodate 360-degree movement and overhead strikes with the weapon. The focus of this training is to complement the close-quarter techniques in Training Objective 22 with kicks and sweeping techniques. You and your training partner should practice each technique, alternating the roles of opponent and defender. The one playing the role of opponent will provide the one executing the technique with moderate resistance to help him master the method.

Standard: Begin the exercise by taking up a position in the middle guard approximately 5 feet from your training partner. Practice all the actions in Training Objective 22 and add either a kick or sweep after each contact.

CHAPTER 17
ASPECTS OF FIGHTING FROM THE GROUND

No martial art or combative training program is complete without addressing the issue of what you do when you are on the ground. This is almost an art unto itself and does require familiarity with some of the grappling and wrestling arts. That said, and in keeping with the fundamental nature of this manual, I am only going to present a very generic set of techniques that should help you get started in this area.

Remember, this territory is different and requires a lot of exploration to be able to apply principles when you are on the ground with a 6-foot staff. Also it is not a matter of *if* you get put on the ground but *when*. That said, we can safely assume that you will end up on the ground due to your own loss of footing or from some action of your opponent. Losing your balance from slipping or tripping when your movement brings you in contact with an environmental aspect will always be a challenge, and it reinforces the need to be very aware of the message of the environment. Let there be no doubt that, when you go down, your opponent will take advantage of the opportunity. Your opponent can also take you down through leg sweeps, kicks, throws, pushes, and even joint locking.

Regardless of how you get there, you will end up either facedown, on your back, or on your side,

and it is from these positions that you must take immediate action to defend yourself and take the fight back to the opponent. The next set of techniques focus on gaining time and position for your primary goal of getting back up.

FIGHTING FROM YOUR BACK

One universal reality of ground fighting with weapons is that it is difficult to fight either face down or on your side. Therefore, the initial goal should be to get either on your back or in a sitting or kneeling position where you can bring your weapon into play. That said, let's look as some of the elements of distance, time, and position associated with being in these positions as depicted in Figure 231. Here two major factors must be considered: the direction of the opponent and the message of the opponent's weapon.

In Figure 231 your opponent is equipped with a staff with a weapons range capability (outer circle) that will allow him to attack you at a greater distance. Basically he can hit you without getting within your range. If equipped with a small weapon (such as a club, sword, or knife), he would have to close to that inner circle, making him vulnerable to both kicks and strikes from the ground. When you're

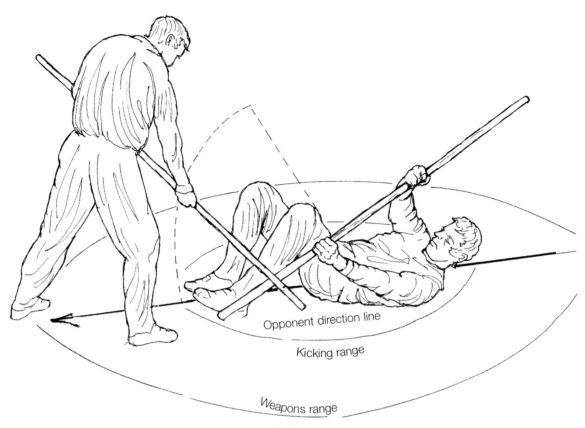

FIGURE 231

on your back, the key is to keep your feet and staff oriented along the "opponent direction line" depicted in Figure 231.

Some ground fighting schools position the feet close together about a foot off the ground, as depicted in Figure 232. Since you look like an upturned turtle in this position, I will call this the "turtleback" position. Although it looks ungainly, from this position you are gaining two additional weapons to complement the staff: blocking and kicking. The legs contain some of the most powerful muscle groups in the human body, and it just makes sense to use them. Also with the knees in this position, they can assist by kicking forward and rolling into the sitting position depicted in Figure 233. From here it is easy to attack and get to your feet by moving through a kneeling position. The following is an exercise for recovering from a fall, returning to a sitting position, and moving into a kneeling position.

TRAINING OBJECTIVE 24

Task: Recover from a backward fall into a sitting position from which strikes and thrusts can be executed.

Condition: You need a staff and training area sufficient to accommodate 360-degree movement and overhead strikes with the weapon. The focus of this training is to recover from a backward fall, rolling through a position on the back and into a seated position. From the seated position, you will execute strikes and thrusts. Later in the exercise you will need a training partner to replicate moderate speed attacks.

Standard: Begin the exercise by taking up a middle-guard position.

FIGURE 232

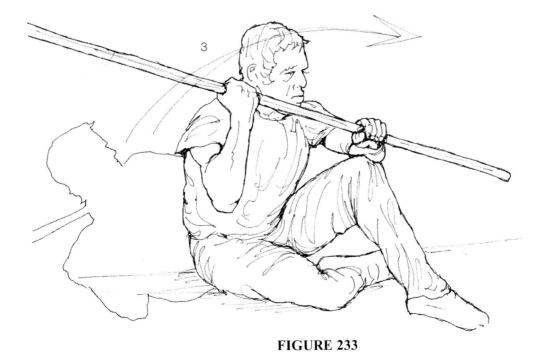

FIGURE 233

Action 1: From the middle-guard position, visualize your opponent giving you a violent shove backward and then simulate your fall by simply sitting down and rolling backward onto your upper back, as depicted in Action 1 in Figure 232. As you roll backward, bring your knees and feet up into the protective posture seen in Action 2 of Figure 232. Immediately rock forward and up into the sitting position shown in Figure 233.

Now, here is an important point: When you hit the ground, your opponent is going to move either to your left or right to gain an advantage and launch his attack. Depending on to which side your opponent moves, tuck that leg under, as shown in Figure 233. For example, as you recover to the sitting position, you see your opponent circle to the right in an attempt to attack your head. Slip your right leg under the left and follow your opponent's movement

around into a kneeling position, as seen in Figure 234. If he moved to your left, then you would tuck the left leg under.

Action 2: Once you are in the kneeling position, execute any combination of strikes or thrusts into Angle 3, 4, 5, 6 and 7 attacks, which were addressed in Figure 36 (page 37). Note that targets within Angles 1, 2, and 8 are not immediately available unless your opponent leans forward or comes within close range.

Action 3: Have your training partner take up a middle-guard position opposite you in a staff-on-staff position. At very slow speed, your partner gives you the same shove addressed in Action 1. In response, take a step backward and then immediately sit down, executing the same roll and recovery described in Action 1. As you return to the

FIGURE 234

sitting position depicted in Figure 233, your training partner will move to his left, circling to find an opening to attack your head. As he begins his movement, follow him around to your right through the sequence depicted in Figure 234. Repeat this same sequence to the opposite side and have the training partner move around to his right.

NOTE: Repeat Action 3 at least 10–15 times at slow speed and then gradually move into full speed.

TURTLEBACK POSITION

Your opponent's speed and movement might enable him to attack you while you are still on your back. When this happens, remember to keep your feet and knees up, facing your opponent. If he attempts to move to the right, use either the staff or your elbows on the ground to pivot in the same direction. If he closes in, use a combination of kicks and strikes to disrupt his attacks. Figure 235 illustrates this.

Strikes and thrusts can be delivered either between or across the top of the knees. It may be necessary to lower one of the knees to intensify impact. Figures 236 and 237 illustrate the approach for striking left and then right while in the turtle-back position. To block for this position, it may be necessary to lower the staff to your leg area, as depicted in Figure 238. Should your opponent strike to your head area, execute the action depicted in Figure 239 while bringing the feet immediately around into the turtleback position. Let's work with this turtleback technique in the following exercise.

Use elbows or staff to assist your turn.

FIGURE 235

FIGURE 236

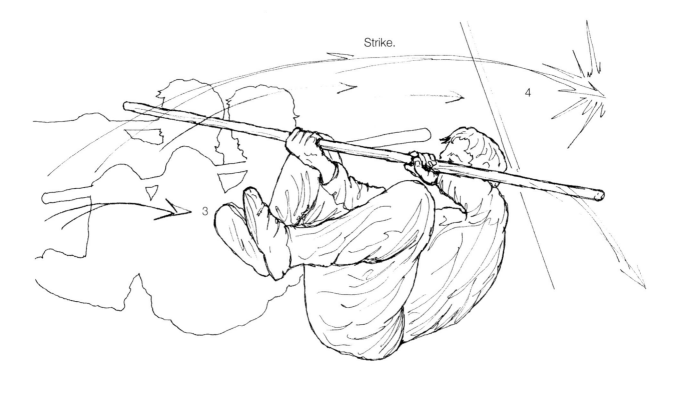

FIGURE 237

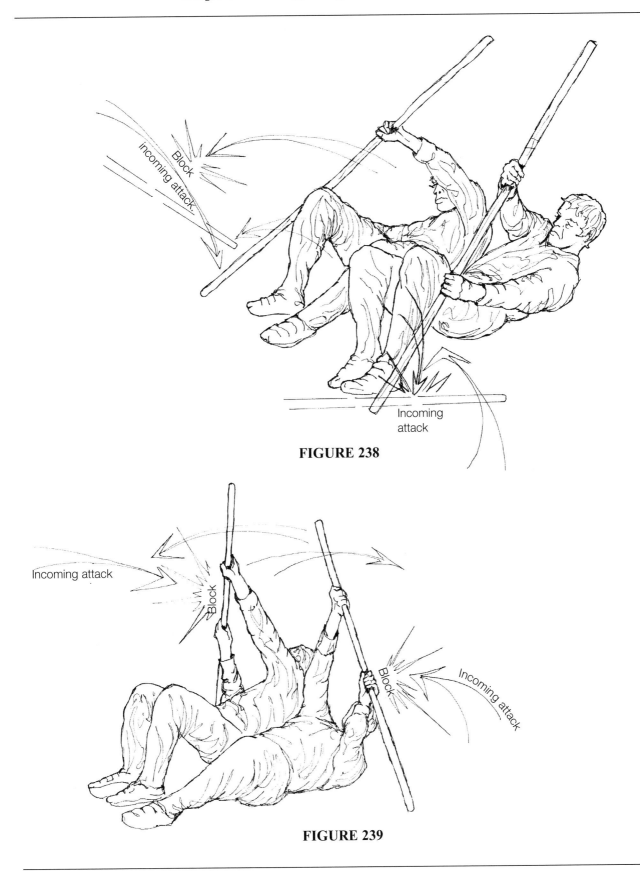

FIGURE 238

FIGURE 239

TRAINING OBJECTIVE 25

Task: From the turtleback position, use both feet and staff to block and attack a moving opponent who is attempting to strike your legs and head.

Condition: You need a staff and training area sufficient to accommodate 360-degree movement and overhead strikes with the weapon. You will also need a training partner to simulate attacks from the weapons range with a staff (Figure 231).

Standard: Begin the exercise by assuming the turtleback position on the ground. Your partner will be circling at weapons range, delivering slow-speed strikes to your lower body and head.

Action 1: Your training partner circles to his right and delivers a strike to your left leg. As in Figure 238, block the incoming strike and then pivot to bring your feet in line with your opponent.

Action 2: Your training partner circles to his left and delivers a strike to your right leg. You swing your staff over and execute the block as shown in Figure 238, immediately following by bringing your feet around in line with the opponent.

Action 3: Your training partner repeats the movements addressed in Actions 1 and 2, only this time he attacks your head. You

FIGURE 240

respond by executing the blocks depicted in Figure 239.

NOTE: Repeat Action 3 from 10–15 times at slow speed and then gradually move into full speed. As you become familiar with this objective, you may add follow-on strikes and kicks to enhance the training benefit.

MOVING FROM A FACEDOWN OR SIDE POSITION

There is always the possibility that you will land facedown. When this occurs, the goal is to get to a seated position as quickly as possible and then onto the knees and subsequently to your feet. Figure 240 demonstrates a simple sequence for accomplishing

this. Remembering to keep your eyes on the enemy, swing either the right or leg over, as in Action 2 on Figure 240, and then immediately slide up into the sitting position, guarding yourself with the staff (Figure 241). Practice this 10–15 times.

FINAL NOTE: Please remember that I have only touched lightly on the many diverse aspects for fighting on the ground with a staff. This topic could be a book in itself. In fact, there are many texts on the market today that address ground fighting, and while they do not specifically address the staff, adapting them to it is worth pursuing. Paladin has many excellent titles on ground fighting that you can check out on its website (www.paladin-press.com).

FIGURE 241

CHAPTER 18
ASPECTS OF STAFF TACTICS

Well, that pretty much wraps up our journey through the fundamentals of staff work. In parting, I would like to make a final comment on some of the tactical methods that are commonly used to deliver these fundamental skills. Some Asian schools execute attacks and defense from the flourishing technique addressed in Figures 32–34. This approach is based on the assumption that the constantly moving staff will confuse or intimidate the opponent and he will not know when or from where the strike will come. It is sort of a buzz-saw effect, which does not always work with every situation.

Another technique seen in some European methods is for the staff to be used more as a polearm, with the staff remaining on the same side regardless of where the opponent is holding his weapon. Some of the medieval and Renaissance masters felt that there was little difference between the longsword and staff techniques and consequently used the staff as if it were a longsword.

All these approaches have merit, and I leave it up to you to research and decide for yourself which approach is best for you. When you look at all these systems and practice with them, the one constant is that the thrust will always be the technique that catches you off guard and disrupts most approaches. Think about it.

REFERENCES AND SOURCES

Agrippa, Camillo. *Tratto di Scienta d'arme.* Rome: Antonio Blado, 1553.

Allanson-Winn, R.G., and C. Phillipps-Wolley. *Broadsword and Singlestick.* Boulder, Colo.: Paladin Press, 2006 (originally published in 1890 by George Bell and Sons, London).

Anglo, Sydney. *The Martial Arts of Renaissance Europe.* New Haven & London: Yale University Press, 2000.

Aylward, J.D. *The English Master of Arms.* London: Routledge & Kegan Paul, 1956.

Di Grassi, Giacomo. *Di Adoprar Sicvramente L'arme.* Venetia: Giordano Ziletti & Company, 1594.

Fiore dei Liberi, *Flos Duellatorum.* Padua, Italy, 1410.

Hatsumi, Masaaki. *Advanced Stick Fighting.* Tokyo: Bunkyo-ku & Kodansha America, Inc., 2005.

Hutton, Alfred. *Cold Steel.* London: William Clowes & Sons Ltd., 1889.

In Hyuk Suh and Jane Hallander. *The Fighting Weapons of Korean Martial Arts.* Burbank, Calif., 1998.

Lindholm, David. *Fighting with the Quarterstaff: A Modern Study of Renaissance Technique.* Highland Village, Texas: The Chivalry Bookshelf, 2006.

McCarthy, Thomas A. *Quarter Staff: A Practical Manual.* London: W. Swan Sonnenschein & Company, 1887.

Mair, Paulus Hector. *A thorough description of the free, knightly, and noble art of fencing, showing various customary defense, affected and put forth with many handsome and useful drawings.* Strasbourg, France, 1570.

Marozzo, Achille. *Opera Nova.* Modena, Italy, 1536.

Silver, George. *Paradoxes of Defense.* London, 1599.

Sutor, Jakob. *Kunstlitches Fechtbuch.* Stuttgart, Germany: J. Scheible, 1849 (reprint of 1612 edition).

Swetnam, Joseph. *The Schoole of the Noble and Worthy Science of Defence.* London: Nicholas Oaks, 1617.

Ting, Leung. *The Ferocious-Enchanted Staff of the Ancient Monks.* Revision of an original manuscript, author unknown. Hong Kong: Leung Ting Company, 1986.

Walker, Donald. *Defensive Exercises.* London: Thomas Hurst, 1840.

Yi Duk-Moo, Park Je-ga, and Pak Dang-soo. *Muye Dobo Tongi (The Comprehensive Illustrated Manual of Martial Arts of Ancient Korea, Date: 1789).* Translation by Sang H. Kim, Hartford, Conn., 2000.

ABOUT THE AUTHOR

With more than 20 years' experience in martial arts, self-defense, and gymnastics, Dwight "Mac" McLemore is certified in kung-fu and expert-level knife combatives, and holds first dan in kendo. *The Fighting Staff* is his fifth book with Paladin Press (*Bowie and Big-Knife Fighting System, Advanced Bowie Fighting, The Fighting Tomahawk*, and *The Fighting Sword*) and the third in his Fighting Weapons series. He is also featured in *The Fighting Tomahawk: The Video*, his firsts video for Paladin Press. He produced the video *Bowie and Big Knife Dueling* in collaboration with Lauric Press and W. Hoch Hochheim; the video has been included in the international curriculum of the Scientific Fighting Congress.

McLemore earned a master's of education degree from Northeast Louisiana State University and has taught physical fitness, gymnastics, and safety/occupational health. He is a retired U.S. Army combat arms officer with extensive knowledge of operations and live-fire training exercises. Retired from a second career as a safety manager with federal civil service, McLemore now works full time developing and writing training support packages in both Western and Asian martial arts. A member of the American Heritage Fighting Arts Association and the Association of Historical Fencing, McLemore founded and directed The School of Two Swords from 1999 to 2007, which provided instruction in edged weapons and self-defense from both Western and Eastern martial arts. He now gives private lessons.

McLemore and his wife, Jeneene, have two grown daughters and one son, and reside in rural Surry County, Virginia, across the river from historic Jamestown.